E-MAIL, THE INTERNET AND THE LAW

Essential knowledge for safer surfing

by

Tim Kevan

Barrister, Middle Temple, BA (Hons) (Cantab)

and

Paul McGrath

Barrister, Gray's Inn, LLB (Hons), (London)

To our parents

In Memory of Paul Sullivan

© Tim Kevan and Paul McGrath 2001

Published by
EMIS Professional Publishing Ltd
31–33 Stonehills House
Welwyn Garden City
Hertfordshire
AL8 6PU

ISBN 1 85811 268 0

Typeset by Saxon Graphics Ltd, Derby.

Cover design by Jane Conway.

Printed and bound in the UK by Antony Rowe Ltd, Bumper's Farm, Chippenham, Wiltshire.

CONTENTS

PART 4: ON-LINE CONTRACTS

PART 5: CONCLUSION

Tim Kevan is a Barrister at 1 Temple Gardens (www.1templegardens.co.uk) with expertise in computer, consumer, employment and personal injury law. He studied economics and law at Magdalene College, Cambridge University and was a scholar of the Middle Temple. In 1993, he was awarded a Young European of the Year Award (Stiftung FVS Joseph Bech Travel Scholarship) by M. Jacques Santer, former President of the European Commission. He has a long-standing interest in the relationship between law and the internet and drafted the Bar's Practice Standards for the use of e-mail by the Bar in 1997. He is the author of the textbook: *A Guide to Credit Hire and Repair: Law and Practice* (1999, CLT Professional Publishing), the Second Edition of which is due in 2001. He surfs and mountain-bikes near his home town of Minehead in Somerset and supports Manchester City. Contact: *timkevan@1templegardens.co.uk.*

Paul McGrath is also a Barrister at 1 Temple Gardens with expertise in computer, employment, consumer and personal injury law. He studied law at London University and was a scholar of Gray's Inn. Contact: *paulmcgrath@1templegardens.co.uk.*

PREFACE

Our aim is to cater for anyone using this medium ranging from the consumer and small businesses to large corporations, lawyers and specialists. It is hoped that this will provide a useful guide to the various areas of law which may impinge on the use of e-mail and other forms of electronic communication and to the nascent body of law which will no doubt soon be recognised as a discrete area in itself. As much as anything it is hoped to highlight some of the potential pitfalls which may beset the unwary and perhaps along the way assuage the curiosity of those taking an interest in this developing field.

It is intended that this will be the first of several editions which will keep up-to-date with on-going developments, and there is an online version with regular updates for advisers (free to purchasers for three months using the voucher at the back of the book).

It should be noted that the examples which have been provided are entirely fictional. Further, they are intended to highlight the issue raised rather than to answer a particular problem.

We have referred to various sources throughout this book. In addition, for more general reference, we would refer the reader to the following books which we have found useful: *Computer Law*, 4th edition, 2000, edited by Chris Reed and John Angel; *Law and the Internet*, 2nd edition, 2000, by Lillian Edwards and Charlotte Waelde; *Information Technology Law*, 3rd Edition, 2000, by Ian J. Lloyd; *The Internet, Law and Society*, First Edition, 2000, edited by Yaman Akdeniz, Clive Walker and David Wall; *Internet and E-Mail Use and Abuse*, 1st edition, 2000, by Clare Hogg; *Internet Law: Text and Materials*, 1st Edition, 2000, by Chris Read; *Butterworths' E-Commerce and IT Law Handbook 2001*, consultant editor: Jeremy Phillips.

The law is stated as it is understood by the authors as at 22 January 2001. Any errors are the authors' own for which we apologise and would hope to correct by the second edition. The purpose of this book is to highlight the various areas of law potentially associated with the use of e-mail. It is not intended to be a substitute for legal advice and readers researching a particular problem should not rely upon its contents in isolation but should instead refer to text-books on the particular aspect of the problem and to legally qualified professionals. All brand and product names used in this book are recognised as trademarks, or registered trademarks, of their respective companies. In particular, Microsoft is recognised as a trademark.

We should like to thank the following people who have helped in the production of this work: Melanie and Sian for their patience and encouragement, Etienne Abrahams for really starting this off with *www.tellmemyrights.com*, Garry Wright for his inspiration and ideas, his invaluable technical advice and for proof-reading, Alex Booth for proof-reading, Hilary Heilbron QC and Steve Gaunt for their legal insight, Michael Pritchett and John McGrath for their technical advice, Tom Hampson, Simon Darling and Benn Finn for their marketing ideas and Andrew Griffin for giving us the opportunity to publish what we believe to be the first such compendium on the subject.

TABLE OF CASES

TABLE OF STATUTES

PART 1: INTRODUCTION

CHAPTER 1

INTRODUCTION TO E-MAIL AND THE INTERNET

"A long time ago, maybe last Thursday ..."

A.A.Milne.

Every society is based upon communication and every major development in a society may be measured by the changes in those means of communication. From the spreading of the gospel by mendicant preachers, to fifteenth century explorers of the high seas, information was dispersed to all corners of the globe. The industrial revolution itself was founded upon developments such as Stephenson's steam locomotive, Telford's canals and the development of turnpike roads. Naturally, these led the way for the formation of the first official postal system using pre-paid stamps and post boxes in the nineteenth century.

THE INTERNET

So it is said today that the development of the internet constitutes the next major change in society as it moves from the industrial to the information age.

Its history begins with the launch of Sputnik by the USSR in 1957. In response, the USA formed a department to establish a lead in science and technology applicable to the military. This led in 1962 to a study on how the USA could maintain its command and control over its missiles and bombers, after a nuclear attack, which eventually resulted in the first electronic network, ARPANET, being constructed in 1969 and the first e-mail program being created by Ray Tomlinson in 1972.

At first used only by the military and academia, it was not until 1990 that the world wide web came into being thanks to Englishman Tim Berners-Lee who, whilst working at CERN in Geneva, implemented a hypertext system to provide efficient information access to the members of the international high-energy physics community. The "www" came into being.

The final piece of the jigsaw came in 1993 when Marc Andreessen developed a graphical user interface to the www called "Mosaic for X" which was the first popular web browser for personal computers. Pictures and graphical documents could then be more easily viewed and cross-referenced on the internet and the commercialisation had begun. Marc Andreessen himself was the first to capitalise on this with the introduction of the Netscape browser and not to be outdone, Microsoft introduced its own Internet Explorer.

Equally as apocryphal as the rise of Netscape and the browser is that of Yahoo! and the search engine. Started in 1994 in a trailer as a student hobby, it went public in 1996 and by 1 March 2000 had a market capitalisation of $83.45 billion. Once again, where Yahoo! went, others followed and there is now a plethora of search engines available which help to sift and organise the information now available on-line.

By September 2000 it was estimated that over 370 million people were on-line world-wide with over 100 million of those in Europe.

The future lies in building upon these developments with, for example, higher speed connections such as ADSL (Asymmetric Digital Subscriber Line) and the convergence of the various forms of media such as television, radio and computers through emerging technologies such as Bluetooth.

E-MAIL

Electronic communications developed alongside the internet. The biggest hurdle to overcome was to get different computers using different operating systems to be able to read each others' messages.

The most significant step in this regard was the introduction of the Simple Mail Transfer Protocol (SMTP) in 1981. The other major development was the introduction of the post-office protocol (POP) which allowed messages to be stored until the user logged on, at which point they are automatically downloaded from the server.

Today, almost all commercial e-mail is sent and received by clients and servers using SMTP or POP3 (the most recent version of POP). However, in recent years there has been an explosion in the use of personal e-mail due to the introduction of web-based services such as Hotmail. These allow the user easy access to their e-mail account from computers other than their own, as well as enabling them to maintain the same e-mail address through changes of service provider.

As well as the technical difficulties, in order to be effective the use of e-mail had to be popularised. Compuserve (now owned by AOL), the internet service provider, for example, was started in 1969 but was not then connected to the internet. They first offered e-mail between Compuserve users in 1979 and real-time chat in 1980. In 1989 they became one of the first two commercial carriers to relay electronic mail to and from the internet. Perhaps most significantly, Hotmail, the free internet-based e-mail service started in 1995.

In a recent study of the internet by UCLA (*www.ccp.ucla.edu*), it was found that some 84% of people on-line have e-mail accounts and over 40% check their e-mail more than once a day.

MOBILE PHONES

Alongside these developments, mobile phone technology developed its own form of data packaging with the development of the short message service ("SMS") which was conceived as part of the Global System for Mobile communications ("GSM") digital standard. This has been followed by the Wireless Application Protocol ("WAP") which provides for limited access to the internet and for the use of e-mail from a mobile phone. Once again, the speed of the connection will be the key and third generation mobiles utilising the Universal Mobile Telephone System ("UMTS") promise to bring the mobile phone into line with other forms of media in this area.

THE LAW

The law is an organic being which has always managed to evolve to keep up with changes in society. However, the challenge posed by the growth of the internet is perhaps its biggest yet not just because of its sheer size, nor the speed with which it has developed. The relationship between law and the internet is based upon a simple conflict:

- laws exist to regulate society;

- the internet has created a new society founded upon the principle that it should be wholly unregulated.

The history of the internet itself is one of decentralisation. Even as far back as 1962, when Paul Baran was commissioned by the US government to study how it could survive a nuclear attack, he envisaged a military research network that was decentralised so that if any locations in the USA were attacked, the military could still have control of nuclear arms for a counter-attack.

Coupled with this has been the romantic idea that the new technologies would form the basis for a true renaissance in learning and culture which would transcend cultural, religious and political boundaries. In one sense the idea represented the apotheosis of the free market, where information is perfect and regulation non-existent.

With this as a backdrop, the law has struggled to keep pace with the new developments and it is no surprise that many legal developments have proved to be controversial. Old legal concepts have been successfully adapted to the new technology but the underlying tension remains: freedom or regulation?

PART 2: EVIDENCE

CHAPTER 2

INFORMATION TECHNOLOGY IN THE COURTROOM

"The way we run our courts has not, in essence, changed for 150 years."
David Lock MP, 'Modernising the Civil Courts, A Consultation Paper',
January 2001

The courts have always tried to keep pace with developments in technology both with regard to the process of the system of justice and the cases that pass through it.

Photographs and visual aids have been used in the courts for decades and television links have been available in the courts for a number of years. E-mail has now been recognised in the new Civil Procedure Rules and it is interesting to note that virtual reality technology has been used during the giving of evidence in the 'Bloody Sunday' Enquiry headed by Lord Saville.

It is unlikely to take very long before all documents in a case are e-mailed to all the parties, along with all of the pleadings, skeleton arguments and even authorities. The advent of secure electronic dealing rooms facilitates just this. Whilst the advent of the photocopier increased the size of the court bundles enormously, the advent of e-mail and electronic storage of documents is likely to reduce this once again.

The following sets out a summary of the various ways that technology (all forms of electronic transmission of information) is currently used in the court process. At the end of the chapter, there is then an introduction to the government's consultation paper on modernising the civil courts. For a more detailed analysis of this area and for thought-provoking ideas for the future, readers are referred to Richard Susskind's two invaluable contributions to the debate: *The Future of the Law*, 1st edition, 1996 (revised paperback edition, 1998) and *Transforming the Law*, 1st edition, 2000.

VIDEO AND TELEPHONE CONFERENCING

Video conferencing is currently little used in the courts. However, provision exists for them to take a greater role in the future.

In criminal cases, section 57(1) of the Crime and Disorder Act 1998 provides:

> "In any proceedings for an offence, a court may, after hearing representations from the parties, direct that the accused shall be treated as being present in the court for any particular hearing before the start of the trial if, during that hearing-
> (a) he is held in custody in a prison or other institution; and
> (b) whether by means of a live television link or otherwise, he is able to see and hear the court and to be seen and heard by it."

This effectively makes it possible for the accused to be tried from his cell although the technology is little used at present.

In civil cases, video conferencing is mentioned in Practice Direction 23.7 of the Civil Procedure Rules 1998 ("CPR") which provides:

> "Where the parties to a matter wish to use video conferencing facilities, and those facilities are available in the relevant court, they should apply to the Master or district judge for directions."

With regard to telephone conferences, CPR Practice Direction 23.6 makes provisions for telephone hearings. In particular, 23.6.2 provides that an order for a telephone hearing will not normally be made unless every party entitled to be given notice of the application and to be heard at the hearing has consented to the order.

It remains unclear how widely video and telephone conferencing will be used in the future as a means of negating the need for attendance at certain hearing. It would seem likely that its use would increase for at least the less controversial hearings such as case management conferences. This is all the more so as video-conferencing in particular gets ever cheaper.

E-MAIL UNDER THE CIVIL PROCEDURE RULES 1998

At present, whilst most solicitors and barristers use e-mail in their practice, the courts lag far behind. Even within the court rules themselves there is very little reference to e-mail. The main provision involves service of documents and later there is a brief reference in the costs provisions.

Service

CPR Rule 6.1(1) provides that:

> "A document may be served by any of the following methods – (e) by fax or other means of electronic communication in accordance with the relevant practice direction."

CPR Rule 6.5(4) provides that:

> "Any document to be served –
> (d) by fax or by other means of electronic communication,
>
> must be sent or transmitted to, or left at, the address for service given by the party to be served."

CPR Practice Direction 6 provides that:

> "3.3 Service by other electronic means [than fax] may take place only where:
> (1) the party serving the document and the party on whom it is to be served are both acting by legal representative,
> (2) the document is served at the legal representative's business address, and
> (3) the legal representative who is to be served has previously expressly indicated in writing to the party serving his willingness to accept service by this means and has provided
> (a) his e-mail address, or
> (b) other electronic identification such as an ISDN or other telephonic link number.
>
> 3.4 Where a document is served by fax or other electronic means, the party serving the document is not required in addition to send a copy by post or document exchange, but if he does not do so and the document is proved not to have been received then the court may, on any application arising out of that non-receipt, take account of the fact that a hard copy was not sent."

At present, these provisions may not appear to be of great significance. However, they do leave the door open for development in the future so long as parties themselves consent.

Effectively, this provides that service may be effected by e-mail so long as both sides are legally represented and the solicitors accepting service have given their e-mail address and consent to be so served.

Solicitors will no doubt start making standard agreements with each other with regard to service by e-mail that will probably become the norm as more solicitors get on-line and the speed of the connections increase.

Costs

CPR Rule 43.4.16 provides:

> "4.16 The following provisions relate to work done by solicitors:
> ... (2) E-mails received by solicitors will not normally be allowed.
> The court may, in its discretion, allow an actual time charge for
> preparation of e-mails sent by solicitors, which properly amount
> to attendances provided that the time taken has been recorded.
> The court may also, in its discretion, allow a sum in respect of
> routine e-mails sent to the client or others on a unit basis of 6
> minutes each, the charge being calculated by reference to the
> appropriate hourly rate."

Given that e-mails promise to be increasingly utilised in the future, it is perhaps surprising that e-mails received by solicitors will not normally be
allowed. This may perhaps be changed in the future. It is at least a start that
time spent on the writing of e-mails will be allowed.

ELECTRONIC TRIAL BUNDLES

In the future it should be possible to have paperless or near paperless electronic trial bundles by the following means.

Correspondence

Most correspondence is typed and saved in a file on the sender's computer. It
is then sent either by e-mail or as a hard copy. As e-mail becomes more popular, the parties will have all of the correspondence saved in electronic form on
their computers.

Authorities

Most authorities are already available in electronic form and with the rise in
prominence of the 'free the law' organisation BAILII much of this is now
available free of charge.

Scanning

Scanners are becoming both cheaper and more powerful and it should not be
very long before all other documents which are not already saved in electronic form are scanned into the electronic case file.

Audio and video tapes

These, too, may quite easily be transferred into digital form and compressed
through, for example WinZip so that they may be transferred between

computers. The development of compression technology in this respect is likely to have a very large effect.

One possibility, which may prove to be a successful business idea in the future, would be for a company to offer streaming facilities to lawyers with access limited to those who are specifically authorised such as the parties and the court. An analogous business at the moment is *www.fotango.com* which not only processes one's photographs but then puts them on-line for the customer and allows access to others for those photographs chosen by the customer for the album. Copies may then be ordered by anyone accessing the site.

File transfer

The transfer of these electronic files and the streaming of audio and video recordings is limited to some extent by the speed of the internet connection. However, many firms are now connected through ISDN and in the next year or so ADSL looks set to take over which will allow enormous files to be transferred and video quality films to be streamed.

This looks set to revolutionise the preparation of cases. Counsel will be able to have access to their solicitors' file. Solicitors will be able to exchange electronic documents and bundles. Searching of files will be speeded up as well as vast savings in paper being made.

CONSULTATION PAPER ON MODERNISING GOVERNMENT

In January 2001, the government issued a consultation paper entitled "Modernising the Civil Courts". A number of the proposals which are made concern information technology and provide a welcome development in the effort to bring the court service into the twenty-first century.

With regard to serving users of the court service or 'customers', they propose:

(a) An increase in choice for customers to communicate with the court through telephone, e-mail, the internet and electronic data interchange.

(b) The provision of interactive on-line services for the convenience of customers.

(c) 'Gateway' partnerships allowing the customer to visit an advisor and link electronically to the court at the same time.

(d) Direct 'Customer Partnerships' which allow regular customers, such as housing authorities, to conduct business directly with the computer systems of the court.

(e) Round the clock services by telephone and internet enabling the customer to conduct business on-line, or to obtain forms and leaflets at convenient times.

(f) The introduction of modern payment methods, such as credit and debit cards, or the development of account services for regular electronic customers.

(g) Internet Services linked to the Community Legal Service, or other government agencies or gateways, and presenting information translated into different languages and that meet the needs of the disabled.

With regard to handling cases and supporting judges and staff, they propose:

(a) The development of the electronic file, enabling practitioners to file documents electronically at court, and for the judge and court staff to work from an electronic case file.

(b) Improved support for judges in the courtroom, including technology to present documents electronically, video links and the digital audio recording of hearings and judgments, extending the work already begun for the Crown Courts into the civil and family courts.

(c) Improved case management through the implementation of electronic diary and case management systems.

(d) Direct access to the record of the court by the parties, and where appropriate the public via the internet.

Unfortunately, whilst the proposals are very much to be welcomed, the timetable for implementation leaves much to be desired. Alongside a number of pilot projects, the timetable is predicted in the following way:

Short term: 12 – 18 months

(a) Development of pilot systems for internet services to support claims issue within 12–18 months. At the same time the first steps will be made to centralise parts of the business building on electronic and telephone services.

(b) Participation in the development of data exchange standards required for the electronic file.

(c) The start of developing or identifying new systems which will support case management and listing activities.

Medium Term: 18 months – 3 years

(a) Start of replacing IT infrastructure.

(b) Continued development of business structures and development and implementation of electronic transactions to support enforcement and case management.

(c) Introduction of primary hearing centres beginning the implementation of courtroom technology in a number of 'pathfinder courts'.

(d) Piloting of technology which supports staff and judges in remote roles, for example bailiffs on the doorstep, or judges at remote locations.

Longer term: 3 years +

(a) Implementation of new services which support the business centres and case management and listing functions and which begin the introduction of the electronic file.

(b) Development of courtroom technology that is integrated with case management systems.

(c) Introduction of procedural change enabling provision of a full range of services in new ways.

These proposals are the logical conclusion of the civil justice reforms started by the Civil Procedure Rules 1998. The keyword all along has been access to justice. However, whilst the rules of procedure have been modernised, the machinery and bureaucracy upon which it was based have lagged behind. These proposals seek to remedy this gap.

The only shame is that that such sensible proposals have been set such a lengthy timetable. The language of the consultation paper is that of business. Customers, regional business centres, partnerships with the private sector – all suggest an approach reminiscent of the private sector. However, the gap between rhetoric and reality is exposed on examination of the timetable. It is hard to imagine any private sector business even of a medium size, never mind one as big as the Court Service, delaying with its IT reforms for so long and hoping to survive. In terms of implementing the service, this begs the single question: would the running of the Court Service better be done in private hands? In other words privatisation. It remains to be seen whether a government would have the political will to introduce such a reform.

CHAPTER 3
E-MAIL SURVEILLANCE: IN EMPLOYMENT AND BEYOND

"Relying on the government to protect your privacy is like asking a peeping tom to install your window blinds."
John Perry Barlow (EFF), 'Decrypting the Puzzle Palace', Communications of the ACM, vol.35, no. 7 (July 1992), pp. 25–31

INTRODUCTION

This chapter sets out an introduction to the law on e-mail surveillance both by employers and by the state and also assesses some of the wider aspects of this subject.

The Regulation of Investigatory Powers Act 2000 (the Act) has replaced the Interception of Communications Act 1985 ("the IOC Act"). The IOC Act was itself in force when, for practical purposes, the only telecommunications were landlines operated by British Telecom. Now the picture is radically different with e-mail, mobile telephones, pagers, internet, intranet, multiple operating companies and ISPs. What with the introduction of the Human Rights Act coupled with all these changes, it is small wonder that the statutory scheme was forced to change.

E-mail surveillance has received considerable recent attention primarily from the employment law perspective. Recent case law and statutory provisions must be considered. This chapter aims to address the issues surrounding the two elements of most importance: (1) the implications in employment law, and (2) the implications of surveillance generally (including the criminal law and human rights).

IMPLICATIONS FOR EMPLOYMENT LAW

The Interception of Communications Act 1985 did not apply to telecommunications systems outside the public network, therefore not forbidding the tapping of private telephone networks. That was successfully challenged in the case of *Halford* v *United Kingdom* (1997) 24 E.H.R.R. 523 where it was held by the European Court of Human Rights that the tapping of the Applicant's office telephone constituted an infringement of her right to privacy under Article 8 of the Convention ("Everyone has the right to respect for his private and family life, his home **and his correspondence**"). The ECHR have made it clear that telephone calls from home and work may be covered by "private life" and "correspondence". In *Halford* the Applicant was not given any notice of any monitoring and therefore had a reasonable expectation that her calls would not be monitored. This was an important factor in the finding that there had been a breach of her right to privacy (supra 543, paragraphs 45–46).

In the commission, the dissenting opinion of Mr H G Schermers identified the fact that the telephone calls made in the office were for office purposes, in the main, and were being paid for by the employer. There would, he said, be possible difficulties in construing such calls as being under the auspices of Article 8 and resulting in those being confidential. He was of the opinion that senior officers were entitled, subject to controls, to supervise telephone calls which have been recorded, for instance. Difficulties also arise where there is an issue as to whether employees are permitted to use the e-mail network for their personal correspondence. This may be especially the case with e-mails with attachments with the increased time and money spent in using the same, but also carrying the risk of viruses.

Given the liability of employers for the e-mails of their staff (see chapters on Vicarious Liability and Defamation), it is small surprise that monitoring is an integral part of good company operation. The extent of the same however is certain to provoke reaction and debate from all concerned.

It is this divide which continues to pervade this area. The current legislation of most note is the Regulation of Investigatory Powers Act 2000, which has repealed and replaced the Interception of Communications Act 1985, and the Telecommunications (Lawful Business Practice) (Interception of Communications) Regulations 2000 SI 2000/2699 (the Regulations).

The Act forbids the intentional monitoring of communications, without lawful authority, by way of a public or private telecommunications system. The inclusion of "private" thereby bringing private employment companies within the Act's scope.

The Regulations came into force on 24th October 2000, almost three weeks after the coming into force of the Human Rights Act 1998. The Regulations provide for the monitoring and recording of defined communications (including e-mail) without the consent of either the sender or the recipient. It should be noted that where the employer has a reasonable belief that both the sender and recipient consent to the interception, then section 3 permits interception. It may well transpire to be the case that employers ask employees in due course to sign consent agreements and in effect to "opt out" in a similar fashion as with the Working Time Directive. It is the author's suggestion that such a provision be incorporated in a policy document relating to the interception of communications (though, of course, both receiver and sender must consent).

Relevance of Communication

The Regulations have been made by the power extended by the Act to the Secretary of State, under section 4(2). They authorise interception only where it is effected "**solely** for the purpose of monitoring or (where appropriate) keeping a record of communications **relevant to the [employer's] business**" (Regulation 3(2)).

> Regulation 2 defines what is relevant to a business. It covers the following:
> "(i) a communication – (aa) by means of which a transaction is entered into in the course of that business, or (bb) which otherwise relates to that business, or
> (ii) a communication which otherwise takes place in the course of carrying on that business".

It can be appreciated from this that the definition is quite wide. It remains to be seen how widely the Regulations will be interpreted but the definition of "course of employment" in cases concerning vicarious liability has been wide. It is doubted that the same width will be applied to the Regulations given the obvious policy differences between the two areas.

Customers and clients are also often friends with the people with whom they do business. The Regulations, it is suggested, will allow monitoring of such e-mails. It may also relate to the business if it is suspected that the employee in question is breaching company policy in some way.

It would appear implicit from the Regulations, the Act and employment law generally that the employer's method and extent of interception will be considered reasonable and lawful only if it is proportionate, objective and fairly applied to all employees.

It must be emphasised that the interception will be lawful under the Act, but that is not necessarily the end of the matter. An employee may, for example, claim discrimination if he is the only person that is monitored despite the legality of the same. Employers should aim to have, and follow, a uniform and proportionate monitoring policy.

To appreciate the possible implications of this area, consider the following. X has a complaint of racial discrimination against Y Co. X brings proceedings in the employment tribunal and is represented by Z Co. X communicates about his case with Z Co by e-mail at his place of employment. Those communications arguably relate to the business as they concern defending legal proceedings against the company. The communications are monitored without his consent. He discovers the same. His legal complaints do not stop at the Act. He has complaints regarding breach of privilege, victimisation, and breach of contract (mutual trust and confidence) at the very least.

Informing the employee

The employer must also have made "all reasonable efforts to inform every person who may use the telecommunications system in question that communications transmitted by means thereof may be intercepted". The making of all reasonable efforts will obviously be judged in context. A large corporate with hundreds of employees at any one given site will take a different approach than for instance a company sharing one office between three employees. In the latter case it *may* be enough to simply tell the others. In the former that would probably not be enough to ensure the message was satisfactorily received by all concerned. It is advisable in any event for employers to ensure that not only do the employees know, but that also they can prove that they have been told and appreciate the significance of the same. It is suggested that some written acknowledgement is completed to avoid allegations at any later stage. This in itself could be achieved by receipted e-mails.

It is clear from the Act and the Regulations that both the receiver and sender are envisaged as having protection. This has great relevance when considering informing both parties. It is easy enough to inform one's own employees but not so for all the customers / friends who may be sending or receiving e-mails.

With regard to the e-mail format it is suggested that the standard form be altered so as to include a reference to telecommunications (including e-mails) being monitored and/or recorded. A similar message would perhaps be prudently added to voicemail and other telecommunications. This would ensure, at least, that the recipient would know before responding that their response would be monitored and/or recorded.

More problematic is regarding incoming e-mails initiated by another who is unaware of the policy. It is suggested that informing such persons would be well nigh impossible in all but the fewest of cases and therefore unlikely to be criticised (establishing contact would be beyond "all reasonable efforts").

When will interception be authorised?

The Regulations allow both monitoring and recording of telecommunications. Recording is obviously a more serious matter than monitoring and hence the Regulations provide for such a distinction.

Telecommunications may only be **monitored** (and not recorded):

(1) "for the purpose of determining whether they are communications relevant to the [employer's] business…"; or,

(2) "for the purposes of monitoring communications made to a confidential voice telephone counselling or support service which is free of charge (other than the cost, if any, of making a telephone call) and operated in such a way that users may remain anonymous if they so choose"

(see Regulation 3(1)(b)(c))

In the following circumstances telecommunications may be **monitored and recorded**:

(1) in order to establish the existence of facts which are relevant to the business (Regulation 3(1)(a)(i)(aa)). An example would be a recording system of e-mails to establish the contractual negotiations entered into with any individual, or a telephone recording system to allow accurate attendance notes to be kept in a firm of solicitors;

(2) in order to ascertain compliance with regulatory or self regulatory practices or procedures which are applicable to the [employer] in the carrying on of his business or applicable to another person in the carrying on of his business where that person is supervised by the [employer] in respect of those practices or procedures (Regulation 3(1)(a)(i)(bb));

(3) in order to ascertain or demonstrate the standards which are achieved or ought to be achieved by persons using the system in the course of their duties (Regulation 3(1)(a)(i)(cc)). This could include, for instance, a call centre determining the appropriate number of calls per day, and setting performance standards from the data;

(4) in the interests of national security (Regulation 3(1)(a)(ii));

(5) for the purpose of preventing or detecting crime (Regulation 3(1)(a)(iii)). Note that "prevention" of crime may be construed to permit monitoring where no crime is suspected at any given time and therefore this element is far wider than if it was merely restricted to "detection";

(6) for the purpose of investigating or detecting the unauthorised use of that or any other telecommunication system (Regulation

3(1)(a)(iv)). This may be against company policy or simply be so gross and excessive so as to amount to a breach of mutual trust and confidence.

(7) for the purpose of the effective operation of the system (Regulation 3(1)(a)(v)). This could include monitoring the introduction of any likely viruses.

The Regulations therefore allow a certain flexibility and it is likely that most businesses will be able to monitor e-mails perfectly legitimately so long as they have proportionality in mind and keep their employees up to date with what is taking place. A private telephone line / e-mail terminal available for employee's own personal use would also indicate proportionality and fairness.

Data Protection and Surveillance

Data protection is dealt with in this work in another chapter, but, it is also of relevance to this chapter. The data on the recorded e-mails may contain data as defined under the Data Protection Act 1998 and require compliance with the same. The Data Protection Commissioner has issued guidance in relation to surveillance (Draft Code of Practice on the use of personal data in employer/employee relationships).

The advice in the guidance can be summarised as follows:

1. set out a clear and useable policy on the use of telecommunications including, perhaps, the number and nature of permitted calls;

2. set out if there is to be any change in the company approach to previous practice (note that the guidance makes it clear that in order to be fair, the practice must be looked at rather than the technical legal position as governed by the contract – if there is a contractual right which has never been enforced, then the employees should be warned if there is to be future enforcement);

3. consider the impact on privacy and autonomy of the individuals who are to be monitored in assessing proportionality and necessity for monitoring;

4. where intending to monitor to protect trade secrets, only monitor where there is a genuine risk of trade secrets being so disclosed;

5. monitor only to the extent required. For example only having random spot checks on possible e-mail abuse and not monitoring all the time;

6. warn employees of monitoring and advise them not to transmit details of which they are sensitive;

7. do not open e-mails that are obviously personal;

8. a need for a virus protection does not warrant the reading of e-mails;

9. provide a way whereby employees can expunge e-mails from their system;

10. make employees aware if their mail box will be opened when on holiday;

11. make sure employees know how much monitoring of the company mobile telephone will take place;

12. provide a personal line for employees to use (even if a payphone).

The general scope and thrust of the guidance is the need for good objective and compelling reasons for surveillance. If surveillance is justified then it should be implemented to the minimal level to achieve the intended goal. At all times there must be good communication between employers and employees.

The guidance should be taken very seriously by all employers, not least because their system may comply with the Act, but may be in contravention of some other duty imposed by law. The arbitrary implementation of a policy could well find employers being sued for discrimination or other such causes of action.

Employers are advised to inform all employees about any proposed changes in plenty of time before the policy is implemented or the practice changed. Where the contract of employment needs amending it is as well to note that generally variations need consent and consideration.

THE CRIMINAL LAW

Regulation of Investigatory Powers Act 2000

"The Act" contains regulation for the following:

(a) interception of communications;

(b) acquisition of communications data;

(c) use of covert surveillance and human intelligence sources;

(d) decryption.

Interception of Communication

This is dealt with under Part I of the Act. As has been seen already (above) the Act has extended the offence of unlawful interception of communications to any communication being transmitted by a public or private telecommunications system.

Section 1 creates both an offence and a civil liability. As we have seen above, section 3 sets out whereby the interception may be lawful without a warrant (i.e. consent, proper operation of the system itself by the operator itself, and certain authorisations under the Wireless Telegraphy Act 1949). Section 5 provides for the authorisation of the interception by virtue of the Secretary of State issuing warrants. The Secretary of State must apply two tests to any application: proportionality and necessity. In order for it to be considered necessary, one of the following must be shown:

(a) that it is in the interests of national security;

(b) that it is for the purpose of preventing or detecting serious crime;

(c) that it is for the purpose of safeguarding the economic well-being of the United Kingdom;

(d) that it is for the purpose of giving effect to the provisions of any international mutual assistance agreement in equivalent circumstances to prevent serious crime.

Proportionality will obviously depend on the facts of the case. However, it is suggested that where there are alternative means of obtaining the information required, the application for a warrant may fail as being disproportionate.

Senior member of police, civil service and other regulatory bodies may apply for warrants (s6). Section 7 provides for the issue to be made, unless in exceptional circumstances, only by the Secretary of State. The warrant must also contain information about who and what is being intercepted (s8).

Section 12 imposes certain obligations upon service providers to maintain a reasonable intercept facility. This will be subject to development and it is too early to predict the width of its application. It seems likely that adequate contributions will be made to the cost of providing such facilities or with the costs of assisting with any investigations (see s14).

Acquisition of communications data

Similar restrictions apply as outlined above. Importantly the strict test of necessity stated in section 22 requires similar factors to be present. It also makes provision for public health, safety and matters such as collection of taxes. Regulation of procedure is similar to the above and dealt with between sections 23 and 25.

Use of covert surveillance and human intelligence sources

This is dealt with under Part II of the Act. There are three subdivisions: intrusive, directed and covert human intelligence sources. They are defined, generally, as follows. Intrusive surveillance is that which takes place at any residential premises or a private car whereby it necessitates some physical presence by either a person or a surveillance device. Directed surveillance is covert and is carried out for a specific operation or investigation and is likely to result in the obtaining of private information where it is reasonably practicable to obtain authorisation before the surveillance. Covert human intelligence sources are people like agents, informants and undercover policemen and do not require further consideration within this work.

For directed and intrusive surveillance, there is no civil liability for acts which are authorised under the warrant granted pursuant to the Act. Again there is the test of necessity which has been referred to above (see sections 28, 29). Any sources must be protected in accordance with section 29.

Decryption

Section 49 enables properly authorised persons (e.g. police, customs and excise and certain members in Crown employment) to serve notices requiring disclosure of protected information in an intelligible form. There are, unsurprisingly, many requirements as to the format of such notices and the ability to obtain the same. The power has caused some concern in the business sector. There are problems, such as the logistical difficulties of the retention and organisation of decryption keys.

The Act is complex and full in its requirements and the analysis of the same would be outside the scope of this chapter. Suffice to say that in the future the courts are sure to be asked to interpret the complex provisions with proportionality, necessity and privacy in mind. The body of case law will be interesting not just to this area of law but to others such as the burden of disclosure in civil cases and the proportionality of the same.

Wireless Telegraphy Act 1949 (as amended by section 73, RIP 2000)

Section 5 makes it an offence for any person to send by wireless telegraphy, or attempt to send, any message which to his knowledge is false or misleading which is likely to prejudice the efficiency of any safety of life service or to endanger the safety of any person, vessel, aircraft or vehicle. It also applies to misleading messages about anybody being in distress or need of help, or indeed the contrary.

It also forbids the using of wireless telegraphy to intercept, or disclose, other messages and information for which he is not authorised to receive (e.g. police radios).

Wireless telegraphy is described as follows:

"(1)…the emitting or receiving, over paths, which are not provided by any material substance constructed or arranged for that purpose, of electro-magnetic energy of a frequency not exceeding three million megacycles a second, being energy which either –

(a) serves for conveying of messages, sound or visual images (whether the messages, sound or images are actually received by any person or not), or for the actuation or control of machinery or apparatus; or

b   is used in connection with the determination of position, bearing, or distance, or for the gaining of information as to the presence, absence, position or motion of any object or of any objects of any class…"

Police Act 1997

The Act allows for the authorisation of covert interception with wireless telegraphy by the police or others. Section 93(7) makes it clear that the Act is supplementary to any existing police powers.

The Act provides the framework by which the police have to operate. It does not deal with the evidential matters such as weight or admissibility.

CONCLUSION

The Act will certainly have a large scale effect upon this area of law. The most interesting developments will probably be the interrelation, and interpretation by the courts, of the guidance given by the Data Protection Commissioner and the wide scope of the Act. As always, human rights will no doubt take centre stage in any legislative interpretation.

CHAPTER 4
USE OF E-MAIL IN EVIDENCE

INTRODUCTION

The problems with the use of e-mail in evidence may be separated into two main categories: admissibility and authenticity. In addition, there are certain special rules which require contracts to be made in 'writing' which may cause some problems with regard to e-mails. This chapter analyses these issues including the use of electronic signatures and the technical problems which may well arise in the future with regard to the use of e-mails in evidence.

ADMISSIBILITY

The main objections with regard to admissibility derive from the nature of the communication. In particular, that the e-mail is not original and further that it is hearsay, in other words, that it is not first hand.

In *R v Governor of Brixton Prison and Another, ex parte Levin* [1997] 3 WLR 117, the House of Lords held among other things that the evidential status of computer print-outs was no different from that of a photocopy of a forged cheque. In general it would therefore be documentary hearsay.

It is not intended here to set out the criminal rules for hearsay and documentary evidence. These may be found in most leading texts.

With regard to civil cases, the situation was made much simpler after the introduction of the Civil Evidence Act 1995. Section 1 of the Act simply abolishes the hearsay rule. Section 8 provides that where a statement in a document is admissible, it may be proved by producing a copy of the document (even if the original is still in existence) and that it is irrelevant what generation of copy the document is.

Section 9 provides that documents which form part of the records of a business (defined very widely) are automatically admissible. A certificate signed by an officer of the business is required under section 9(2) so as to demonstrate that the document forms part of its records and section 9(3) provides that the absence of an entry in those records can be proved by an appropriately signed certificate.

The practical effect of these sections is that subject to the procedural rules, e-mails will be admissible in evidence.

One problematic area in the future may be the use which can be put to evidence which has been obtained illegally, for example, in breach of the Regulation of Investigatory Powers Act 2000.

In *R* v *Khan* [1997] AC 558 the House of Lords had to decide whether criminal evidence amounting to an admission obtained by means of an electronic listening device installed by the police was admissible, and if so whether it should have been excluded under the section 78 of the Police and Criminal Evidence Act 1984 ("PACE").

They held that there was no right of privacy in English law and relevant evidence remained admissible, despite being obtained improperly or unlawfully, subject to the court's discretion to exclude it. *R.* v *Sang* [1980] A.C. 402 followed. Although an apparent breach of Article 8 of the European Convention of Human Rights could be relevant in considering whether to exclude evidence, it was not determinative per se, as an appellant's rights were safeguarded under section 78 of PACE which provided for a review of the admissibility of evidence. A majority of the House of Lords expressed the view that in the instant case it was unnecessary to decide whether a right of privacy existed in English law.

However, that was not the end of the story since the case was taken to the European Court of Human Rights where judgment was given in May 2000 (*Khan v United Kingdom* 8 B.H.R.C. 310; [2000] Crim. L.R. 684; Times, May 23, 2000). Mr Khan had applied to that court complaining that:

(a) his right to privacy under Article 8 of the Convention had been interfered with and that interference was not "in accordance with the law" pursuant to Article 8.2;

(b) there had been a violation of his right to a fair trial under Article 6, given that the only evidence used in the case had been obtained unlawfully; and

(c) he had been denied an effective remedy in relation to his complaints which breached his right under Article 13 to an effective remedy under domestic law.

The Court held unanimously, that there had been a violation of Articles 8 and 13 of the Convention. Mr Khan's right to respect for private and family life had been violated and the interference was found not to be "in accordance with the law" as the phrase required compliance with domestic law. The national rules were unclear being set out only in the non-statutory Home Office Guidelines and therefore the domestic law at the material time did not give protection against interference with an individual's rights. It was not the European Court of Human Right's role to determine whether the evidence was admissible and it found that the secretly taped evidence did not render the proceedings wholly unfair, as the domestic courts could have used their discretionary powers to exclude the evidence under the Police and Criminal Evidence Act 1984 section 78. The criminal proceedings did not provide a suitable remedy or protection from abuse, as the only body to which he could complain about the police surveillance was the Police Complaints Authority. The Court found such an investigation would be insufficiently impartial and therefore Article 13 was also breached (*Govell v UK* (Unreported, January 14, 1998) applied).

Time will tell how this area of law will develop in the light of the incorporation of the Convention into English law. In this context, it should also be noted that in *Douglas and Zeta-Jones and Northern and Shell PLC v Hello! Ltd* [2000] LTL 21 December, Lord Justice Sedley said that the law had to protect those "who find themselves subjected to an unwarranted intrusion into lives". He added, "Mr Douglas and Miss Zeta-Jones have a powerful prima facie claim to redress for invasion of their privacy as a qualified right recognised and protected by English law." For a more detailed analysis of this decision see Chapter 6, below.

ELECTRONIC COMMUNICATIONS ACT 2000

The Electronic Communications Act 2000 ("the ECA") (*gov.uk/acts/acts2000/20000007.htm*) came into force on 25 July 2000 and made the United Kingdom one of the first countries in the world effectively to legalise "e-signatures".

Admissibility

Section 7(1) of the Act provides:

"In any legal proceedings –
(a) an electronic signature incorporated into or logically associated with a particular electronic communication or particular electronic data, and
(b) the certification by any person of such a signature,
shall each be admissible in evidence in relation to any question as to the authenticity of the communication or data or as to the integrity of the communication or data."

The meaning of this is clear. Electronic signatures and associated certification are now admissible in legal proceedings. It is worth noting that this not only includes such signatures incorporated into an electronic communication but also those logically associated with such a communication.

Disputes may arise as to what "logically associated" means. Obviously it will be a question of fact for the particular tribunal but only time will tell what guidance will be given. For example, an electronic signature may have been given in the initial correspondence but not in the final acceptance. It is unclear whether this would count as "logically associated" and it remains to be seen what the courts will make of such a question.

Definition of electronic signature

Section 7(1) clearly begs the question of what is an electronic signature. This is answered in section 7(2) which provides that:

> "For the purposes of this section an electronic signature is so much of anything in electronic form as-
> (a) is incorporated into or otherwise logically associated with any electronic communication or electronic data; and
> (b) purports to be so incorporated or associated for the purpose of being used in establishing the authenticity of the communication or data, the integrity of the communication or data, or both."

Section 7(2)(a) raises the same issues mentioned in the last section with regard to "logically associated". In this instance, however, in order to constitute an electronic signature it merely has to be logically associated with "any" electronic communication or data rather than a "particular" one as mentioned in section 7(1)(a). It should be remembered that in order to come within the Act, section 7(2) must be complied with before even looking at section 7(1)(a).

Section 7(2)(b) provides the substance of the definition. The signature must purport to be so incorporated or associated for the purpose of being used in establishing the authenticity or integrity or both.

Probably in most cases it will be clear that the signature purports to be so incorporated or associated. However, there may be occasions where the intention of the person making the signature will come into question. Once again, this will be a question of fact but no doubt guidance will emerge as the section comes before the courts.

It should be noted that the definition of electronic signature is not limited to e-mails and the internet. Digital signatures can be appended to any document or application form on-screen, off-line as well as on-line.

In theory, the Act should also apply to WAP and SMS. WAP will be easier since it is merely a limited version of e-mail and the internet. However, it may have the difficulty of fully incorporating the signature in the communication.

SMS will not only have the difficulty of limited space and memory but it will also face the evidential problem as to how the signature may be saved. Potentially, it may be down-loaded to a computer although this would be subject to potential verification as to procedures. Alternatively, the Act potentially seems to leave open the possibility physically showing the mobile telephone in court with the message stored therein.

It should also be noted that the signature does not need to be related to the signatories' name. Just as with hand-written signatures, it is not possible to tell someone what theirs should be.

EXAMPLE

Top criminal Barrister Melanie Winter sends an e-mail to a designer label ordering new clothes for her emporium Winter Wonderland. All of the following, if incorporated in the correct way, are capable of amounting to an electronic signature:

    (a) "Melanie Winter";
    (b) "MW";
    (c) "x";
    (d) "Bella"

Certification

Section 7(1)(b) begs the question as to the definition of "certification". Section 7(3) provides that:

> "For the purposes of this section an electronic signature incorporated into or associated with a particular electronic communication or particular electronic data is certified by any person if that person (whether before or after the making of the communication) has made a statement confirming that-
> (a) the signature,
> (b) a means of producing, communicating or verifying the signature, or
> (c) a procedure applied to the signature,
> is (either alone or in combination with other factors) a valid means of establishing the authenticity of the communication or data, the integrity of the communication or data, or both."

Certification is therefore a statement confirming that the signature, the means of producing, communicating or verifying the signature or a procedure applied to the signature is (either by itself or not) a valid means of establishing authenticity or integrity.

Conclusion

It should be noted that just because the electronic signature or certification is admissible it is not necessarily conclusive either to the existence of the contract or as its contents. The particular burden of proof will still need to be passed whether it is the civil "balance of probabilities" or the criminal "beyond reasonable doubt".

Ironically, one of the practical effects of the section on certification is that it may lead to increased questioning as to the validity of the signatures. In any dispute, companies or individuals may be put to strict proof as to the validity of the signature. In many cases this will no doubt be necessary where the authenticity or integrity is in dispute.

However, it is potentially open to abuse by those wishing to unnecessarily complicate or prolong the litigation or simply to increase the other side's costs. Ironically, it may ultimately lead to similar problems originally raised by section 69 of PACE (for which, see below).

This could ultimately lead to an individual needing to come to court for cross-examination on even the smallest and perhaps least controversial of cases. It remains to be seen how the courts will deal with such situations but in the light of the poll tax cases and all the more so with the right to a fair trial under the ECHR, it would seem likely that there will be little that they can do.

Therefore, the Act is not a panacea for all the doubts raised by the new electronic age. Problems such as unauthorised use and forgery will still arise and an electronic signature in this context will not be conclusive. Nor does the Act overcome the jurisdictional or choice of law issues raised in chapter 18.

However, what the Act does is effectively to shift the burden of proof back on the person claiming such unauthorised use or forgery once the other side has jumped the hurdles with regard to certification.

A useful and thought-provoking article on electronic signatures by Stephen Mason may be found at page 37 of the December 1999/January 2000 edition of *Computers and Law* entitled 'Electronic Signatures: The Technical and Legal Ramifications'.

AUTHENTICITY

Prior to 1999, pursuant to section 69 of PACE, in criminal cases evidence from computer records was inadmissible unless conditions relating to the proper use and operation of computer were shown to be satisfied. This hindered the use of e-mails and other electronic evidence since proper use and operation evidence was needed even in uncontroversial circumstances. This was particularly apparent in the numerous cases which appeared in the early 1990s involving those who disputed their poll tax bills.

In order to tackle this problem, the government passed section 60 of the Youth Justice and Criminal Evidence Act 1999 which provided that section 69 of PACE would cease to have effect.

However, despite this, there are many technical issues as to proof which may be raised with regard to the use of e-mail in evidence.

Receiving computer

The first issue is whether the computer which received the e-mail was functioning properly.

In *R* v *Cochrane* [1993] Crim. L.R. 48, the Court of Appeal allowed an appeal against a conviction for theft through the fraudulent use of a cash card. The appeal was on the issue of whether the judge should have admitted evidence in the form of computer printouts or till rolls. The Crown contended that the enquirer's actions in tapping in his request to the cash-point machine rendered the operation akin to a typewriting exercise, so that till rolls produced by the machine were real evidence properly admissible of the transactions which took place. It was held that that ignored the fact that the mainframe computer's role was a sine qua non of any transaction, and of the recording thereof on the rolls. None of the witnesses even knew in which town the mainframe was located. They knew nothing of its operation, and none could say that it was operating correctly at the relevant times. Thus there was a clear gap in the evidence as to how the entries on the cash-point till rolls came into existence. In those circumstances, the judge was unable even to determine whether section 69 of the Police and Criminal Evidence Act 1984 might apply to these till rolls.

Although this was decided under the old law, it does suggest that the computer from which the e-mail is printed may well be relevant if one side is put to proof on this issue. Standard evidence may therefore be needed as to the proper functioning and operation of the particular computer and system.

The other side may question the way the e-mails are stored and how secure such a system is. This would be particularly so where it is denied that a particular individual sent a particular e-mail.

In this context, security of the system may be crucial. Electronic records consist of a stream of numbers, normally in ASCII (American Standard Code for Information Exchange) or some proprietary code representing the letters of the message and possibly control characters defining such things as format and emphasis. When a record is edited, the new version is saved to disk and replaces the old version. The change in the stream of numbers cannot normally be discovered by examining the record itself. (See Chapter 10 of *Computer Law*, 4th edition, edited by Chris Reed and John Angel (Chapter 10 by Chris Reed and Lars Davies)). However, detailed scrutiny of hard discs may in the future help to clarify whether records have been tampered with or not. It is quite possible that software may develop in the future to facilitate this process.

However, whilst there are many potential technical issues which may be raised, in practice authentication may not be so difficult. In *R v Spiby* [1990] 91 Cr App R 186, the Court of Appeal was prepared to presume that a computer was recording evidence accurately when its operator (a hotel manager) testified that he was unaware of any problems in operation, and in the absence of any evidence by the defendant that there was any question of malfunction. This approach was approved by the House of Lords in *R v Shephard* [1993] AC 380.

When making contracts by e-mail, it might be useful to both parties to add a clause clarifying what records each party is expected to keep and further what will be the status of particular records. This may then help in resolving disputes in this area. (See Chapter 10 of *Computer Law*, referred to above).

Intermediate computers

The next stage back are the computers through which the e-mail passed on the way from sender to receiver. In *R v Waddon* [1999] I.T.C.L.R. 422, the court held, among other things, that many computers could be involved in the process of transmitting from sender to receiver via the Internet, both within and outside the jurisdiction involved in the process. However, the intermediate computers were mere post boxes. It was sufficient to certificate the original sending computer and the ultimate receiving computer for the purposes of complying with section 69 and Schedule 3 Part II paragraph 11 of PACE. [In the context of down-loading see also the case of *R v City of London Magistrates Court Ex p. Green* [1997] 3 All E.R. 551.]

However, this line of argument may come under attack where there is a potential suggestion that one of the internet service providers has a bug or where hackers may have penetrated a particular network. If this were to become a common problem, the issue may need re-assessing in the future.

Alternatively, it ma be in some cases that records are kept on intermediate computers, for example, by ISPs. If this is the case and the records are able to be accessed then they may actually help in authenticating e-mails. In this context, it should be noted that commercial organisations have commonly used a system called Electronic Data Interchange ("EDI") for their electronic communications. The EDI log may well provide useful evidence of authentification (See Chapter 10 of *Computer Law*, referred to above).

Sender

Normally, the sender is identified in the e-mail itself. This is the same as with most faxes and telexes. In *Clipper Maritime Ltd* v *Shirlstar Container Transport Ltd (the 'Anemone')* [1987] 1 Lloyds Rep 546, Staughton J, considering whether a telex might constitute a guarantee in writing for the purpose of the Statute of Frauds, said *obiter* (although the point was not relevant in the end):

> "I reached a provisional conclusion in the course of the argument that the answerback of the sender of a telex would constitute a signature, whilst that of the receiver would not since it only authenticates the document and does not convey approval of its contents."

However, it is not difficult for one person effectively to impersonate another through the use of e-mail. Where someone denies sending an e-mail, technical evidence may be needed to prove that the e-mail came from his computer. (It should also be noted that in the case in question there was no dispute that the telex had been sent nor as to its contents.)

In *Takenaka (UK) Ltd and Corfe* v *Frankl* [2000] ILR 11 December, Alliott J unhesitatingly accepted the evidence of a single joint expert that an analysis of the defendant's laptop computer and the e-mail traffic disclosed by it established that the defendant was the author and publisher of a series of admittedly defamatory e-mails.

However, proof that an e-mail came from someone's computer does not necessarily prove that the owner of the computer was the author of the e-mail. Further evidence may also potentially be needed as to the accessibility of the computer and as to its security functions.

Clearly, the use of electronic signatures, cryptography and security passwords would help to prove identification one way or the other.

Deleted e-mails and cookies

E-mails which have been stored on a computer may well end up being discoverable documents in a legal action. This is exactly what happened to Bill Gates in the anti-trust action against Microsoft in the United States.

However, recovery of electronic data may potentially go further than this. Even e-mails which have been deleted by the user may still be tracked down on the hard drive of a computer. On 28 October 2000, Duncan Graham-Rowe reported in the *New Scientist* magazine that:

> "Even if you delete data, whether it's a lengthy document or just a few remarks in an e-mail, those forgotten words could come back to haunt you ... The problem arises because hitting Delete doesn't actually destroy data at all ... The information is still stored on the disc. All that's gone is the map telling the computer where it is ... A mixture of techniques, ranging from simply knowing where to look to high-tech retrieval methods such as scanning tunnelling microscopy, make it possible to dig up a whole host of information from a hard drive or a floppy disc ... Earlier this year a woman was sacked by a British aviation company because e-mails she had sent and subsequently deleted from her Sent Items box had been recovered by her employers, says Brian Palmer a solicitor at the firm Charles Russell in London. Working as a personal assistant, she had been e-mailing her former boss who had left the company to set up his own rival business. She was under the impression that she had removed all traces of the e-mails, says Palmer ..."

At present the retrieval of such information is a time-consuming and laborious job for an expert but one would guess that in time technology will make the process easier.

The problem arises from the fact that people very often treat e-mails like casual conversation whereas the law very often treats them as documentary evidence. The above article reported that an American judge James Rosenbaum in a recent issue of the progressive law journal *Green Bag*, proposed that the courts should no longer be permitted to attach legal value to "cyber trash". At the very least, Congress should pass a law limiting the legal lifespan of deleted data.

An article in *www.theregister.co.uk* on 13 October 1999 reported that the self-destructing e-mail has almost been developed. However, it doubted the full effectiveness of such a system and concluded that, "Probably the best companies can hope for is to increase their ability to reduce information leakage, rather than eliminate it, in which case the documents that are being subpoenaed in current legal actions are still likely to exist, either somewhere with the organisation or with a business partner."

Related to this are the use of 'cookies'. These are effectively markers which are laid down into a user's computer when he visits a particular web-site. They enable the web-sites and those later investigating the use of a computer to see which sites have been visited.

Similar methods of information retrieval can also be used simply to check a company's records. An example of this was reported in *Metro* on 12 January 2001:

> "A disabled boy has won a £1.4 million pay-out amid allegations his computerised medical records were tampered with. The out-of-court settlement was reached after lawyers sent an expert to check the hard drive on computers at the surgery of doctors who treated his mother. He found evidence she was over-prescribe the anti-epileptic drug, Epilim, while trying to get pregnant. However, the records had been amended more than three years later to show a lower, safe dosage had been prescribed. ... The family's lawyer Graeme Swain said the findings had been critical – as they disproved evidence from a computer printout and doctor's hand-written notes. However, he said it had not been possible to identify who had altered the records. ..."

HTML bug

Another method which potentially may be used in the future to track e-mails is the use of what has become known as the 'HTML bug'. The nature of the bug is explained in detail in chapter 10 below. Briefly, it involves embedding a tiny, one-pixel image into an e-mail. Potentially, this may be used like an old-fashioned bug as portrayed in James Bond movies.

In an article on 13 December 2000 in *www.theregister.co.uk*, Thomas C. Greene suggested that the bugs may be used, "for e-mail verification" in which "one might use a simple script to deliver the messages, each containing a unique ID number corresponding to an e-mail address in an existing database." He goes on:

> "Another use for the HTML bug is to track the distribution of documents within a company, e.g., a job-hunter distributing his resume. Everyone who opens the document will automatically connect quietly to the server where the image is stored, and server logs will show who did so.

> For a very sweet dirty trick along those lines, one could embed a link to a porn picture on-line, resized at 1x1 so it's invisible in the e-mail. Network logs will show that a given employee requested, say, *preteen_bestial.gif* from *www.loathsome-sex-offenders.com*. Even better, if the company has spyware in place, the jack-booted network thugs won't even have to be notified by the trickster before grassing him out to senior management."

Wider issues

The use of evidence from a defendant's own computer may face other difficulties such as the right to privacy protected under the European Convention of Human Rights. This has already been dealt with in the previous chapter.

In addition to this, there may be issues such as professional privilege. These are adequately dealt with in the standard texts.

NEED FOR 'WRITING'

If a statute or other provision specifically provides that something must be in 'writing', then there may be problems in fulfilling this through an e-mail. Macdonald and Poyton [2000] 3 Web JCLI (*http://webjcli.ncl.ac.uk/2000/issue3/ macdonald3.html*), in the context of a discussion of section 3 of the Unfair Contract Terms Act 1977 ("UCTA"), question whether section 3 and in particular the word "written" would cover electronic forms of communication. Section 3 provides that an exclusion clause which is part of "written" standard terms of business may only be enforced if it satisfies the reasonableness test.

There is no definition of the word "written" in the Act and they point to Schedule 1 of the Interpretation Act 1978 which provides that "writing" "includes typing, printing, lithography, photography and other modes of representing words in a visible form". "Prima facie", they say, "electronically conveyed information is a series of electronic impulses which, by their nature, are not 'visible' and so not 'writing'."

There are arguments to the contrary. First, it may be said that recorded information is "visible" on the computer screen. Second, if photography is included, it may be argued that this provides a useful analogy since it is only visible after chemical treatment.

In any event, they conclude that any ambiguity is unsatisfactory. The Electronic Communications Act 2000 does not appear to help and they argue that in some way or other section 3 should be clarified by legislation or the courts should adopt a purposive approach in favour of protection.

For the moment, it is unclear how the courts or the legislature will deal with this issue with regard to section 3 of UCTA or in other contexts.

In Chapter 10 of *Computer Law*, referred to above, it is suggested that a provision in an electronic commerce contract which provides that all communications between the parties are deemed to be in writing, and that the use of the prescribed authentication procedures is deemed to be the signature of the appropriate party, may create an estoppel between the parties preventing either of them from denying the validity of an electronic transaction on the ground that the law requires the transaction to have been made in writing.

However, it is pointed out that the estoppel would not bind a third party. Further, it will not be effective if the result would be to declare valid a transaction which is in fact void according to the law for lack of formalities (see, for example, *Swallow and Pearson* v *Middlesex County Council* [1953] 1 All ER 580). This would not be so, however, if the requirement for writing is imposed by the law solely to protect the parties to the transaction, as opposed to the public interest.

By contrast, Reed and Davies argue, the second provision with regard to authenticity stands a good chance of being effective if national law does not specifically demand that signatures be in manuscript form. English law permits signatures to be typewritten or made via stamp (see, for example, *Chapman* v *Smethurst* [1909] 1 KB 927) and there seems no reason to insist on a handwritten signature.

Attention, they say, should instead be focused on the purpose of the signature; to authenticate the message as originating from the purported sender. If this is the correct statement of the function of a signature under English law (for which see, for example, *Goodman* v *J. Eban Ltd* [1954] 1 QB 550; *London County Council* v *Vitamins, Ltd; London County Council* v *Agricultural Food Products Ltd* [1955] 2 QB 218; *Ringham* v *Hackett and Walmsley* (1980) 10 Legal Discussions Affecting Bankers 206; *Bartletts de Reya (A Firm)* v *Byrne* [1983] *The Times* 14 January, 127 SJ 69) then cryptography offers the possibility of producing digital signatures that are more difficult to forge than handwriting.

Finally, Reed and Davies point out that UK legislation contains extensive requirements for writing and signatures (though in general these apply to communications with governmental and administrative bodies rather than commercial communications) and that section 8 of the Electronic Communications Act 2000 confers on ministers the power to repeal many of these provisions. It remains to be seen how this will be utilised.

PART 3: VIRTUAL LIABILITIES

CHAPTER 5

OBSCENITY AND MISUSE OF E-MAIL / INTERNET

INTRODUCTION

This Chapter sets out a brief guide to the laws regulating the issues of obscenity.

With the potential for publication, dissemination and distribution of information over the e-mail network, this area of law is set to change at a speed previously unknown (indeed in *R v C (Stephen)* [1999] 2 Cr App R (S) 154 the Court of Appeal commented that sentencing law may need updating given the internet's powerful scope for commercial exploitation).

This area of law has always been based on morality and the cultural expectations of the public. The internet has now created a worldwide fully interactive web for the mutual interchange of ideas, information, beliefs, and opinions. With that comes the inevitable varying degrees of acceptability. Once standards are set at a particular level there is then the question, perhaps the most difficult, of enforcement. This chapter is intended to review the law and its applicability to the use of e-mail both in the workplace and at home.

COMPETING RIGHTS: FREEDOM OF EXPRESSION AND PRIVACY

Never before have fundamental freedoms and rights been so important. The enactment of the Human Rights Act 1998 ("the HRA") has brought with it a set of rights which aim to protect and liberate society. Within that wide ambit there is ample scope for conflict.

Under Article 8 of the ECHR (and now found in Schedule 1 of the HRA) "Everyone has the right to respect for his private and family life, his home and his correspondence" (presumably, correspondence will be interpreted widely, as has family life: *K v UK* (1986) 50 DR 199).

Under Article 9 everyone has the right to "freedom of thought, conscience and religion". "Thought" is obviously a wide concept and will cover not just recognised religions. Indeed it is wide enough to cover all types of "atheists, agnostics, sceptics and the unconcerned" (see *Kokkinakis* v *Greece* [1994] 17 EHRR 397). However, it is not as wide as the ordinary dictionary definition may suggest. The European Court has not been willing to see it expand to cover purely political goals.

Each person has the unqualified right to hold a particular belief or to hold certain thoughts. However, the manifestation of the same is subject to the restrictions of article 9(2). Under 9(2) it is expressly provided that "Freedom to manifest one's religion or beliefs shall be subject only to such limitations as are prescribed by law and are necessary in a democratic society in the interests of public safety, for the protection of public order, health or **morals**, or for the protection of the rights and freedoms of others".

This inevitably raises a potential conflict which the courts will have to resolve in each case. The balancing exercise must be carried out by each contracting state. It is almost certain that each government will interpret the same differently.

Under Article 10, everyone has the right to freedom of expression. This will have critical implications for e-mail and the internet. With the millions of e-mails sent everyday from every location, it is not difficult to imagine how important this freedom may transpire to be. The exercise of such freedoms may be "subject to such formalities, conditions, restrictions or penalties as are prescribed by law and are necessary in a democratic society, in the interests of … the protection of health and morals". Therefore there again exists a critical distinction between the right itself and how it may be manifested and controlled.

It will be interesting to see how the courts approach this area of law in the field of e-mail and the internet. The access to multifarious web-sites allows an increasing audience access to millions of pages of information. These can be transmitted literally at a click of a button by e-mail.

OBSCENITY, INDECENCY AND RELATED TOPICS: THE COMMON LAW

Though now largely regulated by statute, obscenity and indecency laws have their roots in the common law. In relation to obscenity there is now a statutory bar to prosecution for a common law offence "where it is of the essence of the offence that the matter is obscene" (s2(4) Obscene Publications Act 1959). That aside there is no restriction to prosecution for the common law offences relating to indecency or immorality. Importantly, as regards e-mail, the offences of conspiracy to outrage public decency, conspiracy to corrupt public morals, and outraging public decency have been preserved. Therefore, agreement to publish, as opposed to actual publication, remains live at common law.

Outraging public decency consists of exhibiting anything in public which outrages public decency. It does not have to be "obscene" in order for it to be indecent (see *R v Stanley* [1965] 2 QB 327). Obscenity is seen as a more serious matter and therefore has a higher threshold.

It can be instantly appreciated that the internet reaches a vast public audience. In sending materials a user must therefore be careful as to the documents and attachments that he/she sends. It is important to note that outraging public decency is not restricted to any specific categories. For instance the sale of ear-rings made from human foetuses was held to be indecent in *R v Gibson* [1990] 2 QB 619.

The act itself must be objectively indecent. It will not be enough to merely show that there was some indecent intent. However, the lack of intention to be indecent is not a defence once it has been shown that there was a deliberate act which resulted in something which was objectively indecent. Unlike with obscenity, there is no possible defence of justification.

Conspiracy is shown once there is an agreement between two or more to commit an act which amounts to public indecency.

Conspiracy to corrupt public morals is based upon the protection of public standards. As the mutual interchange of ideas, customs, cultures and traditions passes between people with increasing rapidity and as society moves on to a more liberated and tolerant state, it is likely that the jurisprudence in this area will develop. Public morality will obviously be judged at the time when the issue is raised. For instance, what offended public morality in the Nineteenth Century may well not offend public morality in the present day.

Given the vast amount of information available over the internet, users must be conscious of the legal implications in this area, similarly, the judiciary will almost certainly be forced to rethink the status of the law and regulation in this area. In *Shaw v DPP* [1962] AC 220 it was held that a directory of prostitutes met the required standard and the offence of conspiracy to corrupt public morals was established. It undermined family and moral values. Lord Reid, in dissent, concluded that extending the boundaries of the criminal law was a matter for Parliament and not the courts. However, the courts must now be alive to the fact that Parliament are going to find it almost impossible to keep up with the developments of the internet and the problems that this will bring. The courts must assume a pivotal role in order to assure that the spirit of the law is applied consistently and that the mischief of the statutes are enforced.

STATUTORY REGULATION OF OBSCENITY AND INDECENCY

By far the most significant statutory regulation is that contained within the Obscene Publications Act 1959. The test for whether an article is obscene under the Act is whether "the effect of any one of its items is, if taken as a whole, such as to tend and deprave and corrupt persons who are likely, having regard to all relevant circumstances, to read, see or hear the matter contained or embodied in it" (section 1). Section 2 makes it an offence to publish any obscene article. By section 1(2) the Act catches within its province anything to be read or looked at, any film, any sound recording, or any other record of pictures. Given the wide public scope of the Act there is, following recent case law (for which see below), no doubt that materials sent via e-mail will be within its ambit (indeed by the Criminal Justice and Public Order Act 1994, the statute was amended to extend publication to expressly include where the matter is data stored electronically on the transmission of that data: see section 168(1) Schedule 9, para. 3).

The question as to what is, or is not, obscene is obviously one of fact and degree. For instance a pornographic book circulated to young children will undoubtedly fall within the definition. However, the same material solely available to adults, is unlikely to be viewed as having the same effect. It is important therefore to consider this matter further in the virtual world. Access to e-mail can be obtained by anybody with access to a computer and a telephone line. Access to certain internet sites is not difficult. Without proper regulation materials can be obtained from the source and circulated to a wide audience. This poses a twofold question: (1) to what extent should the law interfere and regulate? and (2) how is it to be enforced?

Given that the audience is potentially so large and hard to place limits upon the assessment of obscenity may not be limited to the intended audience but rather the *actual* or *potential* audience.

This has received some limited recent attention in the courts. In *R v Waddon* [1999] I.T.C.L.R 422 the defendant had obtained images which had been created out of the jurisdiction and transferred to a number of different web-sites via an internet service provider (ISP). The defendant argued that publication had occurred abroad and consequently fell outside the jurisdiction. On this point, Judge Hardy found that section 1(3)(b) (i.e. the section relating to publication) included (a) where data had been electronically stored and also (b) the transmission of the data. Following on from that he found that the information was published when transmitted by the defendant to his agent and to the ISP. It was therefore sent and received in the jurisdiction and the publication was complete.

The defendant appealed to the Court of Appeal. The Court of Appeal held that publication could take place when loaded on to a website abroad. Publication took place again when the information was downloaded in a different location. A statement on a computer screen was similar to that contained within a document and consequently the information was published. As to whether the material is "made" or not – see below.

Protection of Children Act 1978

Under section 1(1) it is an offence, inter alia, to make an indecent photograph of a child under the age of 16. The definition of "make" could have critical implications for the sanctity and effectiveness of this measure (including ramifications for other areas of law). For instance if "make" is to be viewed restrictively so as to mean the actual taking of the photograph with a camera, this would give limited protection to children. The illicit industry could transmit pictures which could be passed on between individuals and differing jurisdictions. It could soon become the case that despite a huge proliferation of such photographs, there is no offence committed within the jurisdiction. This would plainly defeat the wide policy behind the Act. The wider view would construe "make" as including creating an image by downloading or otherwise.

This question reached the Court of Appeal, albeit in a different guise, in *R v Bowden* [2000] 2 WLR 1083. The Court of Appeal held that "to make" must be given its ordinary dictionary meaning. This included the storage of images on disks and hardware by virtue of section 7 of the Obscene Publications Act 1959. Therefore downloading did amount to "making". This shows that there is a distinction to be made between the original creator and the subsequent makers of the photograph. The section is to be construed widely. Interestingly it was held that *each* download amounted to the making of *new* material. This decision, it is respectfully submitted, is plainly correct. The policy of the Act must maintain effectiveness and continuity through the changing world of information dissemination. Without such flexibility the court would have to wait for Parliament to change and amend statutes at the same rate of speed as the development of e-mail and the internet as a whole. This was the sentiment expressed in *R v Fellows* [1997] 2 All ER 548 reciting *AG Ref (No. 5 of 1980)* (1980) 72 Cr App R 71, and *Longmuir v HM Advocate* 2000 J.C. 378 (where under a similar statutory provision downloading indecent photographs amounted to "making" them).

In relation to the form of the data, *Fellows* is also authority for the proposition that the form of the material is also not to be restrictively construed. Section 7 of the Act (which defines photographs, films and pseudo photographs) is not to be viewed as imposing any limitation as to the form of the information. It followed that section 7 was wide enough to cover later forms of photographs and copies of such photographs.

Regarding the related offence of possession of such photographs under section 160 Criminal Justice Act 1988, it has also been made clear that the storage of the information on computer amounted to an offence. In *Atkins* v *DPP* [2000] 1 WLR 1427 it was held that "making" included copying, downloading, or storing it on a computer *so long as it was stored knowingly*. This is important. For instance consider that an e-mail is sent by X to Y with an attachment of material which would be regarded as indecent. Y is not at the workstation when the material is received by his computer and has no previous knowledge regarding the same. At this stage, *Atkins*, along with section 160(2(b)), would be authority that Y has committed no offence. When Y returns to the workstation, Y sees the e-mail with an attachment. There is nothing in the e-mail to suggest the contents of the attachment. At this stage, again, it would seem that *Atkins* is authority for the proposition that no offence has been committed by Y. Then consider Y downloads the attachment. The images are transported to his workstation and are displayed on the monitor. Y is then in possession – has he committed an offence? The position under more conventional situations has been resolved so as to afford a defence if the person had received the matter unsolicited and had not kept it for an unreasonable time (see section 160(2)(c)). What amounts to a reasonable time will be a question of fact and degree, but with the e-mail network being as rapid response as it is, it will not be surprising if any length of time over and above that which was reasonably necessary to delete the same will be permitted. It is suggested that in the normal course of events, saving the information for any reason other than informing the authorities (or possibly the employer of the sender) would be keeping it for an unreasonable time.

Another ambiguity in this regard arises from the system of temporary internet files. This automatically stores material from the internet in temporary files. It requires no extra act from the user. It is arguable that this may also constitute storage in this regard.

Atkins also covered an interesting side issue. That is, whether two photos taped together is to be viewed as a photograph or pseudo photograph. It was held that it would not be so construed. However, a reproduction of that image may well amount to a photograph.

A further measure designed to protect children is the Children and Young Persons (Harmful Publications) Act 1955. This aims to punish people who publish, or distribute, any matter which consists mainly of cartoons that depict violence / horror / crimes which would tend to corrupt a child into whose hands it was likely to fall. The prosecution has to be brought by the Attorney General. Again, with the internet expanding and reaching an extraordinary audience, presently little-used legislation may well take a front row position in the regulation of cyberspace.

The American Perspective: Reno v ACLU

Several years ago, in the USA, concern began to mount regarding the easy accessibility to internet porn and other unsuitable material for children. Given the increasing use and availability of the internet for children it was seen that legislation should step in. This was enacted in the form of the Communications Decency Act 1996. Effectively the statute sought to regulate and criminalize the distribution of unsuitable material over the internet.

This was challenged by a variety of civil liberties groups and resulted in a hearing before the Supreme Court (521 US 844 (1997)). The pertinent provisions were quashed by the Supreme Court. The Court were of the view that sufficient safeguards existed to prevent children being inadvertently exposed to unsuitable material. In any event the importance of the freedom of expression outweighed the other factors. This remains the current position in the US despite another legislative attempt with the Child Online Protection Act. This was similarly frustrated by court action.

The internet seems, in the short term at least, to be heading for self regulation with perhaps State led codes of conduct. It remains to be seen the effectiveness of the same (see further chapter 14 on vicarious liability).

The French and German perspective: reaching out into cyberspace

The recent decisions of the national Courts in France and Germany have caused some controversy. The two decisions have a differing degree of significance.

In Germany the Courts held that the national laws against the denial of the Holocaust and the spreading of Nazi propaganda apply to the internet. This was so even where the content originates from another country and from a non-German. Liability was restricted to individuals with their own web-sites. Thus ISPs were not affected.

In the now infamous Yahoo! case the French Courts reached even further. The proceedings were issued against Yahoo! Inc. (based in the US) for the contravention of similar French law. Yahoo! contested jurisdiction on the basis that they were based in the United States. The French Courts then received the opinion of experts as to whether Yahoo! could block the site to French traffic. Apparently Yahoo! could block approximately 90% of such traffic. The Court held that they had jurisdiction over the case and then went on to hold that Yahoo! must take all measures to stamp out the possibility of the sale of such material.

Whether this type of judgment will have any effect will depend upon the ability to enforce a French judgment in the US. Yahoo! is, according to an article by Ian De Freitas (*The Times*, 9 January 2001), seeking a declaration from the US Courts that the judgment not be recognised in the US. This is not an issue about the impropriety of Nazi memorabilia, but instead the extent and nature of regulation and which court has the jurisdiction to determine matters relating to unsuitable material on the net. For obvious reasons Yahoo! and other ISPs are concerned about the extent of their potential liability should this type of judgment be enforceable. Enforcement of foreign judgments is an extremely complicated issue and outside the scope of this work. However, this area is sure to provide hotly contested litigation in the future and similar cases will no doubt emerge.

Video Recordings Act 1984

This statute was enacted so as to enable the enforcement of proper video classification. It makes it an offence not to have a classification certificate for any video recording. Some videos are exempt from classification (e.g. educational videos).

Computer games do not have to be submitted to the BBFC unless they contain material which is likely to require classification. There is a voluntary rating system for computer games run by the European Leisure Software Publishers Association.

In *Kent CC* v *Multi Media Marketing (Canterbury) Ltd* 94 L.G.R. 474, the defendant company did not have a classification certificate from the British Board of Film Classification. The article in question was a computer game with a quiz element. That part of the game did not involve any moving images. On successful completion of the game, it would display a short clip of moving naked women. The case stated to the Divisional Court dealt with the following questions: (1) was it a video recording under section 1? (2) was it to be seen as a video game and therefore exempt under section (2)(1)(c)? and (3) would it be within the sexuality provisions of section 2(2)?

The court held that: (1) the short clip following the game was a video work as it had a continuous moving picture. It could be severed from the rest of the material; (2) as the short clip was separate from the game, it could not be exempt; (3) even if the whole was to be viewed as a game, then it was not exempt as it depicted female genitalia and was therefore to be viewed as showing, or encouraging, sexual activity.

What with the increase of games being circulated and extracted from the internet, this case cannot be ignored. The courts are obviously willing to look into the substance of the game and to assess whether the scene truly is part of the game, or in fact is something else.

Post Office Act 1953

By section 11 it is an offence to send any obscene or indecent article. "Obscene" under this statute has its ordinary meaning which includes lewd and indecent and does not have the more restricted meaning as under the Obscene Publications Act 1959.

At present, most materials are sent by e-mail with attachments. It will be interesting to see whether there will be any legislation to apply the sentiment of the Post Office Act to the internet and e-mail network. The Post Office Act cannot apply given that it is limited to items sent by post with the postal service. It does however, seem to be the case that if a disk containing indecent matters was sent via the postal system, an offence would be committed.

Telecommunications Act 1984

By reason of section 43 it is an offence to send by means of a public telecommunication system a "message, or other matter that is grossly offensive or of an indecent, obscene or menacing character...". Section 4 makes it clear that "telecommunications system" means a system

"for the conveyance, through the agency of electric, magnetic, electro-magnetic, electro-chemical or electro-mechanical energy, of – (a) speech, music and other sounds; (b) visual images; (c) signals serving for the impartation (whether as between persons and persons, things and things or persons and things) of any matter otherwise than in the for of sounds or visual images; or (d) signals serving for the actuation or control of machinery or apparatus".

The effect of this section has not yet been fully investigated with relation to e-mail and to functions such as text messaging. It is sure to expand the possibilities of punishment. There is likely to be a conflict, certainly in the short term, between Article 10, European Convention of Human Rights and these provisions now that the Human Rights Act 1998 is in force. The plateau will probably be reached by a compromise between justified restrictions by reason of the protection of morals, and by reason of the fact that enforcement is likely to be very difficult and hence reserved for the most serious cases.

A recent example of the application of this statute to mobile telephone text-messaging was reported in *The Times* by Alan Hamilton on 1 November 2000:

"Jealous husband fined over text messages

A SCOTTISH farmworker was convicted yesterday of the new crime of sending offensive text messages on a mobile telephone. Callum Boyce, 23, a father of two, was fined £100 by Perth Sheriff Court for using the technology to send grossly offensive messages to a colleague's phone after finding him alone with his wife. After receiving four messages on his phone within half an hour, Peter Buller contacted police and Boyce was arrested. He was charged under the Telecommunications Act, 1984, which prohibits obscene messages on mobile phones. Although other convictions have involved mobile phone text messages, yesterday's case is thought to be the first based solely on offensive language in such a message. The court was told that Mr Buller knew who had sent the messages, because Boyce's number flashed on the display panel of his mobile phone. The two men, both of Milnathort, Perthshire, used to be friends but now worked on neighbouring farms and no longer had any contact with each other. Rosie Scott, solicitor for Boyce, told the court that while Mr Buller was on sick leave, Boyce got his job on the farm, and there was aggravation between the two men when Mr Buller returned to work. "The final straw came when the accused returned home from work and found Mr Buller in his house. Boyce's wife said he had been making advances, suggesting she should have sex with him," Mrs Scott said. "Mrs Boyce was clearly upset, and her husband decided he had had enough." Some of the messages he sent included foul and suggestive language. Others read: "Are you still paying for sex?" and "Baldy pervert, you have wrecked our marriage, so I am going to break your neck." Text messages have become hugely popular in the past year, especially with teenagers. A year ago an estimated 50 million messages a month were being exchanged in Britain; by August the number had risen to half a billion. But besides being an easy way for teenagers to communicate, they are also an easy tool for harassment – especially by school bullies."

Currently, text messages are not as broad a medium as e-mail and the internet. However, similar issues arise in relation to regulation and it remains to be seen how the technological advances of text messaging and mobile telephones will involve the law in this area.

EXAMPLE

England footballer Dominic Adamson receives a text message from an admiring fan. As he scrolls down it contains a joke about surfing which he finds funny and so he immediately forwards the message to his friends Brad Cousens and Greg, Glen and Jenny Millward at the Spot Backpacker in Umtentweni, South Africa. Unknown to him (since he had not scrolled down the full message), the message also contained an obscene picture at the end which was also forwarded.

Has he thereby committed an offence under the Telecommunications Act 1948?

Public Order Act 1986

The Act provides a general prohibition on public order offences such as riot or harassment. By virtue of amendment (see for example, section 31 Crime and Disorder Act 1998), it has become an offence to cause fear, or harassment which is racially aggravated.

It is an offence to use "towards another person threatening, abusive or insulting words...or distributes or displays to another person any writing, sign or other visible representation" with intent to (1) cause another to believe that immediate unlawful violence will be used against them or (2) to provoke another into violence (see section 4). Such an offence may be committed in a public "or private place". However, of most importance is the provision that there is an exception where it is distributed by a person in a dwelling and the other person is also in a dwelling. "Dwelling" will probably not include anybody's place of work (see section 8). As a result a defence would not apply to those using their office computers, or indeed internet cafés or other such facilities. Similar provisions apply to intentional harassment, alarm or distress (section 4A).

Use of words, display of written material and the publication / distribution of material which is intended or is likely to stir up racial hatred will also amount to an offence (see sections 18 – 23 of the 1986 Act).

This will be important when groups which are racially motivated use the internet to disseminate material or to organise marches, etc. The creation of the offence is obviously welcome. However, the enforcement of the law will prove difficult given the anonymity of the internet.

Recent cases have applied the law widely:

In *Rogers and others* v *DPP* LTL 22/7/99 it was held by the Divisional Court that a person could be guilty of the offence if it could reasonably be inferred that the defendant intended to cause harassment, alarm or distress to another by his activities. It was not necessary to prove that the defendant knew that the victim was at the scene or that the victim would experience any of the alleged disorderly behaviour.

In *CPS* v *Weeks* ILR 17 July 2000; LTL 5/9/2000, the Divisional Court held that intention was a question of fact, however, that the absence of awareness that the words may have been threatening, abusive or insulting was immaterial.

Users of the internet and e-mail system will be well warned to avoid any messages or communications which may be determined as being offensive in some relevant way. E-mail is simply another medium by which users can harass others. The ease of the communication will no doubt increase the use of this statutory provision.

Computer Misuse Act 1990

This Act creates three new offences:

1. unauthorised access to a computer ("hacking", section 1);

2. unauthorised access to a computer with intent to commit or facilitate the commission of a serious crime (section 2) and

3. unauthorised modification of computer material (section 3).

Access is defined as unauthorised if "(a) he is not himself entitled to control access of the kind in question to the program or data; and (b) he does not have consent to access by him of the kind in question to the program or data from any person who is so entitled" (see section 17(5)). The offences can be committed by insiders or outsiders. The offences may also be committed where access is made to data of a particular kind (irrespective of whether there is authority to enter other data using the same system). However, an "...employee should only be guilty of an offence if his employer has clearly defined the limits of the employee's authority to access a program or data..." (per Lord Hobhouse, *R* v *Bow Street Magistrates ex p. US Govt* [1999] 3 WLR 620 at 629G).

Hacking

An offence is committed where a person:

(a) causes a computer to perform any function with intent to secure access to any program or data held in any computer;

(b) the access he intends to secure is unauthorised; and

(c) he knows at the time when he causes the computer to perform the function that that is the case.

The intent need not be directed at (a) any particular program or data; (b) a program or data of any particular kind; (c) a program or data held in any particular computer (see section 1(1)(2)).

Also, it is important to note that an offence is committed whether the data is accessed directly from the computer holding the data, or indirectly accessed by using another computer: see *A-G's Reference (No. 1 of 1991)* [1993] QB 94 where it was held that the words "causes a computer to perform any function with intent to secure access to any program or data held in any computer" were not confined to the use of one computer with intent to secure access into another computer. Thus if a person intentionally caused a computer to perform a function to obtain unauthorised access to, for example, data, contained within the same computer, an offence will still be committed.

Hacking with intent to commit / facilitate serious crime

An offence is committed if any person, commits computer hacking (as defined above) with the intention to commit a relevant offence or to facilitate the commission of such an offence (whether by himself or by another). The relevant offences are listed as those which carry a fixed sentence by law or those which someone over 21 might be imprisoned for 5 years or more (ignoring the effect of section 33 of the Magistrates Court Act 1980). The offence may be committed even where the commission of the further offence is impossible.

This section is obviously more serious than that under section 1 and carries with it a maximum of 5 years' imprisonment.

EXAMPLE

Jewel thieves Kathryn Baker and Lucy Sullivan are planning to burgle a bank. Lucy Sullivan says to Kathryn Baker that it would be easy if they could find a way in after hours. Kathryn Baker hacks into the computer records of Matt Waddams (Surveyors) at its site office in London looking for plans which indicate any structural openings or weaknesses in any bank. The surveyors keep all of their structural plans on their network of computers at the international head office in Minehead. While Kathryn Baker is searching the London office she finds a link to the Minehead network. Using this link Kathryn Baker discovers the plans for Simon Darling Bank PLC. She takes copies of the plans and e-mails them to Lucy Sullivan. Lucy Sullivan breaks into the bank and steals £1,000,000. She is caught and the Police discover Kathryn Baker's involvement.

Kathryn Baker is probably guilty under section 1 because she has caused a computer to perform a function with intent to access data held in a computer. She knew that this was unauthorised access. By virtue of section 1(2) it will be of little use for her to argue that she did not know where and how the data was stored. She will also probably be guilty under section 2 because she intended to facilitate Lucy Sullivan's burglary.

Unauthorised modification

An offence is committed where a person:

(a) does any act which causes an unauthorised modification of the contents of any computer; and

(b) at the time when he does the act he has the requisite intent and the requisite knowledge.

The "requisite knowledge" is simply that he knows that the modification he intends to cause is unauthorised.

The "requisite intent" will be shown where there is an intent to cause a modification of the contents of any computer and by so doing to impair the operation of any computer, to prevent or hinder access to any data or program or to impair the operation of any program or to impair the reliability of any data. The intent does not need to be directed at any particular computer. It also need not be directed at any data, program, or modification or data, program or modification of any particular kind.

As a side issue, it is not criminal damage as defined under the Criminal Damage Act 1971, unless there is physical impairment of the computer or the computer medium's condition (see section 3(6)).

Importantly the definition of computer has been left open by the statute. This is no doubt to allow the courts to move with the technology and not be fettered by technical definitions which may become redundant or of limited effect.

The courts have jurisdiction where the offences are committed abroad. Thus the internet or other such network is not a means of escape. There are limited exceptions, for which see section 4.

CONCLUSION

This area has a large scope for great expansion due to the internet. The courts will have to be alive to the multiplicity of issues, rights and freedoms in attempting to strike the correct balance. The strongest competing factors will be the aim to protect society on the one hand and freedom of expression on the other.

CHAPTER 6
DEFAMATION

"The Net interprets censorship as damage and routes around it."

John Gilmore (EFF), NYT 1/15/96

INTRODUCTION

This chapter sets out a brief introduction to the issues of defamation and breach of confidence in this area.

DEFAMATION

The issue of defamation by e-mail has received much coverage recently, following the British Gas/EGS settlement in the UK and the on-going Microsoft anti-trust law suit in the US.

In the British Gas case, a former employee of British Gas set up a rival company to the British Gas subsidiary, Transco. The case apparently hinged on an e-mail circulated by a British Gas manager who alleged that there was a 'high level complaint' against the former employee, and at the same time instructed British Gas staff to have no further dealings with him. The case was settled out of court.

The Microsoft case highlights the permanence of the seemingly 'off the cuff' remark, if sent by e-mail. Excerpts from internal messages sent by Bill Gates to his employees have ended up as evidence in the anti-trust suit to support allegations that Microsoft used its Windows monopoly to force competitors out of the market.

This chapter sets out the basic ingredients of the law of defamation and concludes with a review of the *Defamation Act 1996* and recent case law.

GENERAL

> "The right of every person, during life, to the unimpaired possession
> of reputation and a good name is recognised by the law"
> *(see* Clerk & Lindsell On Torts, *Eighteenth edition, Sweet & Maxwell at*
> *22–01).*

The right to one's reputation is intangible but fundamental, and ranges from an individual's personal life to the protection of a large body-corporate and its trading-base built from its goodwill.

Though people often refer to matters being defamatory, the tort is by far from a simple area of law. Indeed a libel action currently holds the record for the longest running civil trial in English history (*McDonalds Corporation* v *Steel* [1995] 3 All ER 615) and this is a good indication that more is at stake than personal reputations. Whether it be financially stratospheric or a matter of personal pride, defamation via the e-mail is an important subject which cannot be overlooked.

As discussed elsewhere in this work, the right to freedom of expression will no doubt conflict and intermingle with the right not to be defamed. In *Derbyshire County Council* v *Times Newspapers Ltd & Others* [1993] AC 534, the House of Lords held that a local authority had no right to sue in libel to protect its governing or administrative reputation. Such a right, it was held, would be contrary to the freedom of expression under Article 10 of the ECHR and would place an unreasonable restriction upon the expression of public opinion.

THE CONSTITUENT PARTS OF DEFAMATION

Every individual and corporate has their right protected by the tort of defamation. The only requirement is that there must be a legal personality that can be defamed (for public policy reasons, political organisations cannot bring an action for defamation: see *Goldsmith* v *Bhoyrul* [1997] 4 All ER 268). As a result companies can sue in their own name for the protection of, for example, their goodwill built upon reputation. Defamation includes both slander and libel. Slander is a defamatory statement which is transient in nature. Libel indicates a statement which has some degree of permanence. It is not necessarily restricted to text and has been held for many years to include matters such as film recordings: see *Youssoupoff* v *MGM Pictures Ltd* (1934) 50 TLR 581. Libel is actionable *per se*, whereas for slander it must be proved that the slander resulted in some actual damage (save for some limited exceptions).

E-mails are recorded data transmitted from one machine to another. They can incorporate text and pictures, be printed out, saved on to disk and treated very much like a standard document. It is therefore the case that they have some degree of permanence and will be regarded, if fulfilling all the other requirements, as being libellous, as opposed to slanderous. For this reason, this chapter does not consider slander in any more detail.

E-mails are an unusual cross between conversation on the one hand and letter writing on the other. This brings with it the dangers that people will not word e-mails as wisely as they would a letter, and yet, the e-mail, with its degree of permanence becomes a potentially libellous document and subject to the same scrutiny as a letter (and therefore actual damage does not have to be proven).

The motive of the person making the defamatory statement is not relevant in determining primary liability (though see *Defences* below). There are two primary questions which must be answered: (1) did the statement have a defamatory meaning, and (2) did it refer to the complainant?

Defamatory Meaning

In relation to the first issue, the test is what the words would reasonably be understood to mean in the light of the surrounding circumstances as known to the person to whom they were published. In this regard it is important to remember that it makes no difference that certain facts were not known to the maker of the statement which would put a different complexion on the statement had they known. The only test is objective – was it defamatory? In testing whether it is defamatory the court must consider factors such as whether it would "lower the [complainant] in the estimation of right-thinking members of society generally" (see *Sim* v *Stretch* (1936) 52 TLR 669 at 671) or shunned and avoided (see *Clerk & Lindsell* supra. 22–19). The essence of the tort centres around someone's integrity and right to a reputation. It is therefore important to note that the facts of the case are very important and therefore a statement may, in one instance, be defamatory, and yet in another, not be so.

Importantly, mere abuse will not usually amount to defamation. The reasonable meaning of the words is crucial. Words that merely convey insults, do not generally amount to a defamatory meaning. The same may not be true in certain circumstances. Consider for example the well known case of *Tolley* v *Fry* [1931] AC 333. There, a chocolate company had pictured a golfer implying that he ate and supported the advertisement for chocolate. This was held to be capable of a defamatory meaning. At first this may seem unusual. However, the golfer was of amateur status and not allowed to receive funds for sponsorship. The advertisement implied that as he was supporting the advertising feature, he would have received funds for the same. This put his moral and ethical standing as a legitimate amateur golfer in some doubt to reasonable thinking members of the public.

The publication must be considered as a whole and not merely parts in isolation. In *Charleston and another* v *News Group Newspapers Ltd and another* [1995] 2 WLR 450 two TV personalities were superimposed by a technical process on to the image of a pornographic scene. The article went on to criticise the computer program which enabled such editing and superimposition. The action foundered on the basis that it was clear that the persons concerned did not consent and that the article taken as a whole was insulting but not defamatory. The submission that the whole of the article need not be considered and that a section of the public would only read the headlines and therefore take away a defamatory meaning failed. Their Lordships held that such a reader would not amount to being an "ordinary, reasonable and fair minded reader" (per Lord Bridge at 456 C).

Words or other materials may possess a defamatory meaning not just by what they expressly or impliedly say, but also by innuendo. The complainant will then have to show what the words are truly meaning. This will often involve the complainant adducing evidence of the full factual background to enable the court to adjudicate upon the issue, not in a vacuum, but with the full picture set out for it.

Reference to the Complainant

The next issue is satisfied if the defamatory matter would reasonably be understood by members of the public who knew the complainant to refer to him. It matters not whether they were in fact referring to the complainant.

It is for the complainant to show that he has been referred to. However, it is irrelevant what form that takes. Importantly for e-mail users, is the point that reference by initials, or fake names, can suffice (see *Roach* v *Garvan* (1742) 2 Atk. 469 and *Youssoupoff* v *MGM Pictures*, above, respectively). In addition any reference which by inference refers to the complainant will be enough.

Publication

In order for an action for defamation to arise, the statement must be published, either intentionally or negligently. In this regard it is important to appreciate that once negligence or intention has been shown, it is irrelevant that the statement was published mistakenly to someone other than the intended recipient. This is so even if the original recipient was intended to be the complainant alone (see *Fox* v *Broderick* (1864) 14 Ir CLR 453, and *Clerk & Lindsell*, supra. at 22–73/4). Whether the publication is negligent depends on the facts of the case. If the maker of the statement sent it marked "private and confidential", by post, then it could be a defence to show that someone else reading it was not foreseeable. However, if it is not so marked, then it could be seen as reasonably foreseeable that another would read it and consequently liability would follow: see *Theaker* v *Richardson* [1962] 1 WLR 151.

The tort is predicated upon reputation and this means what the members of the public think of any individual. Thus where X sends an abusive letter to Y, there is no publication as the matter is strictly private between them. Unless there is some other communication, the members of the public will never find out about it.

EXAMPLE

Miss Sian Owen is a world class film actress. In 2001 she accepts three film engagements filmed in various locations around the world. As she is constantly on the move she uses e-mail to keep in touch with her agent, John 'The Wolf' Lovekin. Miss Owen often takes part in charity galas and is well respected in such fields as a generous benefactor. When discussing contractual negotiations, over the e-mail system, he describes her as "being too greedy" and refers to her charity work as "a front to mask your selfishness". John Lovekin forwards all communications to his personal assistant, Ali Cornish, for filing. The allegations are not true and have been motivated by friction between Miss Owen and John Lovekin.

The allegations are personal between Miss Owen and John Lovekin. However, on the transmission of the communications to Ali Cornish, it is likely that they have been published. They now take the form of a libellous statement and are actionable *per se*. The comments are likely to be defamatory given that they are plainly not true.

It can be appreciated that simply with a click of the button, e-mails can become forwarded, and thereby published, documents. This is not the case where it can be shown that

    (a) the original maker of the statement authorised or intended for there to be a repetition,

    (b) where the repetition was the natural and probable / foreseeable consequence of the original statement (see *Slipper* v *BBC* [1991] QB 283), or

    (c) where the person to whom the original statement was made was under some duty to repeat the statement.

People who are merely messengers of defamation, where they could not reasonably have known about the same, are not responsible (so, for instance, postmen do not "publish" the letters that they deliver). Persons that fail to remove defamatory material may, depending on the facts, be publishers. It was said in *Byrne* v *Dean* [1937] 1 KB 818 at 837 that the test was "having regard to all the facts of the case, is the proper inference that, by not removing the defamatory matter, the defendant really made himself responsible for its continued presence in the place where it had been put" (per Greene LJ).

From the above it is readily appreciable that e-mail and the internet will complicate matters in this area. The most notorious case at present in this area is *Godfrey* v *Demon Internet Ltd* [1999] 4 All ER 342. There, the defendant was an internet service provider (ISP) who offered a Usenet facility enabling persons to publish material to readers across the globe. Persons would submit their work (postings) to the local service provider who would then disseminate them via the internet. The defendant's Usegroup facility kept the articles for two weeks. On 13th January 1997 an article was posted which was purportedly written by the claimant. It was a forgery and defamatory of the claimant. On 17th January the claimant informed the defendant of the forgery and asked that the matter be removed. The defendant did not remove the entry until the expiry of the two week period (i.e. 27th January). The claimant brought proceedings alleging defamation for the period between 17th January and 27th January. The defendants argued, inter alia, that they were not the common law publishers.

Morland J. held that the Defendants were indeed common law publishers:

> "In my judgment the defendant, whenever it transmits and whenever there is transmitted from the storage of its news server a defamatory posting, publish that posting to any subscriber to its ISP who accesses the newsgroup containing that posting. Thus every time one of the defendant's customers accesses "soc.culture.thai" and sees that posting defamatory of the plaintiff there is a publication to that customer" (at 348e-f).

The defendant had submitted that the they were merely the owner of an electronic device through which postings were transmitted. However, Morland J. rejected such a submission pointing to the fact that the defendant stored postings within its computers and could be accessed on that newsgroup. Further, the defendant had sufficient control to obliterate the postings when it felt so necessary. The decision is of fundamental importance to ISPs. It also shows the wide construction being applied to publication in the internet field. The lack of a passive role was important in the finding that there was active publication, this can be distinguished from where mere technical equipment is used: see for example *Anderson* v *New York Telephone Co* (1974) 35 NY 2d 746.

The American authorities were reviewed in some depth but then swiftly dealt with by stating that the American law and English law were different in approach and therefore the cases were of limited persuasiveness. This case acknowledges that the internet, and information on it, is not merely provided by mechanical processes. The ISPs are to be seen as living operations with control, and ultimately responsibility, over the material that they provide.

An example of a settlement by virtue of alleged e-mail defamation can be seen by virtue of *Exoteric Gas Solutions Ltd and Andrew Duffield* v *BG plc* (1999, unrep). In that case, following a former employee setting up a company in related activities, there was an alleged defamatory message sent in an e-mail asking employees to have no dealings with the claimants. The trial did not go ahead due to a settlement. These allegations are typical of what can be expected in the future and it is clear that e-mail and the law of defamation have clearly a significant future together.

There is a further element to publication. A person who *procures* another to publish a defamatory statement will be liable: see *Parkes* v *Prescott* (1869) LR 4 Ex 169. Procurement will be a question of fact.

OTHER IMPLICATIONS FOR THE INTERNET

We have already seen that ISPs can become liable for defamation. There is no sanctity from this area of law and as such all organisations should tread carefully. Newsgroups, the USENET and discussion fora are all vulnerable to attack. Given the extraordinary speed with which postings can be distributed across the globe, this is a worrying concept and one which must be guarded against (see Lilian Edwards' discussion, chapter 11, *Internet and the Law*, 2nd edition, 2000).

Postings may well be anonymous and as a result the publishers of the statements are the only ones identifiable to be sued. An example of the same is a recent American case reported by Robert Blincoe in *www.theregister.co.uk* on 11 December 2000:

"Dr bags $675k in Net libel case

A US doctor has won an Internet libel case, which his lawyers believe is the first judgement based on an anonymous Net message. Dr Sam Graham was awarded $675,000 last week. Graham used to work at the Emory University School of Medicine. In February 1999 he discovered a posting on a Yahoo! message board which reckoned he had taken kicks backs in his old job when he gave his department's business to a urology company. The posting was made by 'fbiinformant'. This turned out to be Dr Jonathan Oppenheimer who had worked at the urology company. The judge called the Internet messages "about as despicable as any course of conduct that one could engage in." ®"

Restriction of allegedly defamatory postings may be complicated by the global nature of the internet. In *Macquarie Bank* v *Berg* [1999] NSWSC 526 an employee set up a web site which posted allegedly defamatory material concerning an Australian bank on an American server. Access to the same was, of course, worldwide. The Australian court refused to restrain publication because, inter alia, the restraint would lead to an imposition of Australian libel law on the world (i.e. preventing access to the site in a country where the information concerned would not amount to defamation).

ISPs have also been the subject to US litigation in the cases of *Cubby* v *CompuServe* 766 F Supp 135 (SD NY 1991), and *Stratton Oakmont Inc* v *Prodigy Services* 1995 NY Misc., 23 Media L. Rep. 1794. Both cases considered the liability of ISPs where the alleged dissemination was "innocent" and where there was a third party to edit and control material. Both cases, unfortunately, were decided differently. In the former case the court held that given the lack of control that the defendant exercised it acted merely as a public library or other such innocent intermediary. In the latter case the court held that there was no such protection as the site had put itself out as being family orientated and that it would control the information put out on its site. Given the speed with which the internet has moved on, it is not certain whether either case would offer great assistance in any case that fell to be decided in today's climate.

THE DEFENCES

There are essentially 5 defences to a claim for defamation:

1. Justification (or truth);

2. Absolute privilege;

3. Qualified privilege;

4. Fair comment;

5. Section 1 Defamation Act 1996.

Justification or Truth

It will be a defence if the Defendant can prove that each fact as alleged is substantially true. The nature of the allegedly defamatory statement will dictate the nature of the justification required and admissible. For instance, if X is alleged to have stolen jewellery from a store on New Bond Street, it will not be justified by evidence that he has convictions for jewellery theft (putting aside the issue of admissibility: see chapter 4). However, if the allegation was that X was dishonest and not to be trusted, then the evidence may well justify the statement. In each case it is a question of fact and degree.

In addition each statement may contain different, and separate, allegations of a defamatory nature. Where there is more than one defamatory allegation, each must be justified. This is subject to section 5 of the Defamation Act 1952 which provides that justification can be made out where, despite not justifying all the allegations, the reputation of the complainant is not materially affected given the other justification.

Absolute Privilege

This operates as a complete defence to any defamation proceedings. The defence is concerned with judicial proceedings, parliamentary proceedings and official business.

In judicial proceedings before any court or tribunal recognised by law, there is no cause of action for words said within those proceedings, no matter whosoever shall say them. Similarly, communications about the litigation between solicitor and client attract absolute privilege. It remains to be seen what the approach will be to items such as reports / comments from judges on the judicial intranet.

The same applies to any statement made in the course of parliamentary proceedings, or in the course of official business of public servants. In relation to parliamentary proceedings there is now an option for the person concerned to waive the privilege (see section 13 Defamation Act 1996).

Qualified Privilege

This operates as a defence to proceedings and consists of:

(a) limited statements between persons with a common duty / interest to make *and* receive such statements (or in the public interest);

(b) statements made to the public pursuant to some form of duty (legal, social or moral, or in response to a public attack);

(c) fair and accurate reporting of specified proceedings.

The list is not exhaustive as it is founded upon public policy. In addition to the above, it must be shown that the statement was made at a fit and proper time (to be judged objectively), that the statement referred to the occasion in question and that it was published under right and honest motives. All three need be shown. Thus it must be shown, importantly, that the communication was privileged and that the occasion was privileged. Thus it can lead to a certain statement being privileged to one section of the public, but not to others (see *Chapman* v *Ellesmere* [1932] 2 KB 431).

In an employment relationship there is a positive duty for employees to inform employers of all matters within their care. For instance, an e-mail to a disciplinary panel regarding the conduct of one of the employees under investigation will usually be privileged if made without malice and at the proper time. Similarly, employers may attract qualified privilege in keeping their employees informed on important matters relating to their employment. An employer would be privileged in warning fellow employees about another employee. However, the mere relationship of employment is not enough to justify the exchange of defamatory statements about others in the organisation. There must always be a direct interest in the making of the statement. For instance, a complaint regarding one of the fellow employees should be made to the line manager (or other suitable person) and not simply a colleague with no responsibility for the same. The range of confidential relationships whereby the privilege may be attracted is not exhaustive and it will depend upon the facts in question.

There is also limited protection for self-defence. Self-defence is where the defamatory statement is made in response to a defamatory attack or where the defamatory statement is made to justify one's own position.

In a similar vein as qualified privilege, there operates the defence for fair reporting of judicial proceedings, Parliamentary proceedings, and public hearings and meetings. The essential elements are very similar to qualified privilege, in that the report must be fair and accurate and that it must not be motivated by malice. It is a defence to the repetition of defamatory statements. If the fair and accurate report of court proceedings is made contemporaneously, then it will attract absolute privilege: see section 14 Defamation Act 1996.

In *Albert Reynolds* v *(1) Times Newspapers Limited; (2) Alan Ruddock; and (3) John Witherow* [1999] 3 WLR 1010 it was held that there was no separate head of qualified privilege for political information. The common law test should therefore be applied as is normally the case. Importantly their Lordships, in the majority, held that "the elasticity of the common law principle enables interference with freedom of speech to be confined to what is necessary in the circumstances of the case. This elasticity enables the court to give appropriate weight, in today's conditions, to the importance of freedom of expression by the media on all matters of public concern" (at 1027B). Proliferation of media materials over the internet is of course affected by this and other cases concerning the intertwining of freedom of expression, defamation and what is in the public interest.

Fair Comment and Criticism

This is a general right to express otherwise defamatory opinions on any matter of public interest. It has always been seen as one of the essential aspects of free speech, this can only be strengthened by the recent incorporation of Article 10 of the European Convention on Human Rights under the Human Rights Act. This freedom to express defamatory *opinions* must not be confused with statements of defamatory *facts*, only the former is permitted. Again, the comment must be made without malice to afford a defence.

The publication of a statement of another, where there is no reason to doubt the honesty of the other's statement, will generally afford a defence: see *Telnikoff* v *Mateusevitch* [1992] 2 AC 343.

To qualify as fair comment the statement must be based on facts which are substantially true, or honestly believed to be true and themselves protected by privilege. It also must relate to the area with which there is a genuine interest as opposed to simply assailing an individual on unrelated grounds. For instance, it would be permissible on a book review web-site to say that a book was immoral, however, it would scarcely be so if the posting said that the author, personally, was so immoral.

In addition to the four main categories of defence is the statute-created "offer of amends". Under sections 2 – 4 of the Defamation Act 1996, if an offer of amends is accepted, then it shall act as a bar to proceedings (save as for enforcing the offer of amends with the appropriate financial compensation as agreed, or determined by the court). If the offer is not accepted (and not withdrawn) then it is a defence if the person making the offer knew or had reason to believe that the statement referred (or was likely to be understood to refer) to the complainant and that it was both false and defamatory. This has practically rendered the old defence of "apology" redundant.

In *Celestine Babayari* v *Express Newspapers* (LTL 24/7/2000) the defendant published an alleged defamatory report on its web site. The defence was that of fair comment. The case was settled with damages and an apology in open court for any distress or embarrassment that it may have caused to the claimant. The case is a good example of the fact that postings on web sites can remain in circulation, whereas newspapers (for example) can be viewed as being more transitory. The flip side, of course, is that to remove an article from a web site is far easier than to recall an edition of a national newspaper.

Section 1 Defamation Act 1996

This has been considered, in part, when dealing with publication, above. Section 1 provides:

> "(1) In defamation proceedings a person has a defence if he shows that (a) he was not the author, editor or publisher of the statement complained of, (b) he took reasonable care in relation to its publication, and (c) he did not know, and had no reason to believe, that what he did caused or contributed to the publication of a defamatory statement.

(2) For this purpose ... "publisher" have the following meanings, which are further explained in subsection (3) ... "publisher" means a commercial publisher, that is, a person whose business is issuing material to the public, or a section of the public, who issues material containing the statement in the course of that business.

(3) A person shall not be considered the author, editor or publisher of a statement is he is only involved – (a) in printing, producing, distributing or selling printed material containing the statement ... (c) in processing, making copies of, distributing or selling any electronic medium in or on which the statement is recorded, or in operating or providing any equipment, system or service by means of which the statement is retrieved, copied, distributed or made available in electronic form...(e) as the operator of or provider of access to a communications system by means of which the statement is transmitted, or made available, by a person over whom he has no effective control. In a case not within paragraphs (a) to (e) the court may have regard to those provisions by way of analogy in deciding whether a person is to be considered the author, editor or publisher of a statement...

(5) In determining for the purposes of this section whether a person took reasonable care, or had reason to believe, that what he did caused or contributed to the publication of a defamatory statement, regard should be had to – (a) the extent of his responsibility for the content of the statement or the decision to publish it, (b) the nature or circumstances of the publication, and (c) the previous conduct or character of the author, editor or publisher."

Godfrey v *Demon Internet Ltd* (above) is authority for the proposition that all three elements have to be proved in order to afford a defence. Morland J. was of the view that the defendant was "clearly not the publisher of the posting" under these sections. This was no doubt heavily influenced from the wording of subsection (3)(c).

EXAMPLE

Exmoor Beast hunter Richard Waddams runs guided tours about the beast. French tourist Arnaud Leroux does not believe that the beast exists and posts a message on a Somerset Tourist Board web-site notice-board stating that Richard Waddams is misleading tourists into a false belief in this respect. The web-site is hosted by the ISP Michael Pritchett Communications PLC. Richard Waddams complains to the tourist board and the ISP that the message is defamatory.

Who is the publisher: Arnaud Leroux, the web-site or the ISP?
Who would have the burden of proof on the existence of the beast?
Can the ISP rely upon section 1 of the Defamation Act 1996?

Evidential Matters

Putting the theory into practice is sometimes not as straightforward as one might hope. The complex nature of the internet and e-mail systems can enable many to stay anonymous. It is then a question of tracing the individual concerned and taking appropriate action. In *(1) Takenaka (UK) Ltd (2) Brian Corfe* v *David Frankl* ILR 11 December 2000; LTL 1/11/00 the issue at stake was whether the defendant had been the author and publisher of defamatory statements contained in e-mails regarding the first and second claimants. The e-mails were traced, by means of a single joint expert, to a laptop. The expert concluded that the author was "most probably" the defendant. The judge accepted such a finding. The costs of the pre-litigation search for the author and publisher was allowed (following a concession).

The company received general damages of £1,000 (limited it would appear, due to the fact that it was not an individual) and the individual received damages of £25,000. Given the persistent denial of the offence a permanent injunction was granted. Costs were awarded on an indemnity basis.

It is suggested that as soon as litigation is considered, those seeking to claim should inform the other party that all e-mails should be retained and not destroyed. This will prevent excusable deletions and the consequent lack of evidence facing the proposed claimant.

CONCLUSION

Now with the Human Rights Act importing Article 10 into all Law, it is imperative for all concerned to consider very carefully as to the nature of a communication and their interest in making it to the persons concerned. Given the increasing number of documented statements in the form of e-mails, it is likely that evidence that would have been previously lacking, will be available for inspection by any proposed complainants. Their authors are well advised to consider carefully the content of any e-mail which will not be judged by what they meant, but rather what it means to the reasonable person. Thus "jokes" or matters "not to be taken seriously" may attract serious repercussions not just for their authors, but for all vicariously responsible for them (see chapter 14).

The recent American case discussed at page 65 highlights the need for caution.

BREACH OF CONFIDENCE/PRIVACY

Even where a statement in a particular e-mail is true, it may still potentially constitute a breach of confidence or privacy.

The law in this area has developed from the equitable jurisdiction whereby the judges of the Court of Chancery restrained freedom of speech in circumstances in which it would be unconscionable to publish private material. If information is accepted on the basis that it is kept secret, the recipient's conscience is bound by that confidence and it will be unconscionable for him to break his duty of confidence by publishing the information to others (*Stephens* v *Avery* [1988] Ch 449, 556).

However, "there is no confidence in inequity" and the cases show how, on occasion, the courts were willing to permit publication, on that or other grounds, even though the information was originally given in confidence (see, for example, *Fraser* v *Evans* [1969] 1 QB 349, 362 and *Hubbard* v *Vosper* [1972] 2 QB 84, 95 and 101).

In *Argyll* v *Argyll* [1967] Ch 302, Ungoed-Thomas J granted the Duchess of Argyll an injunction restraining her former husband from publishing information about her in breach of confidence one partner to a marriage (or other intimate relationship) owes to another. *Michael Barrymore* v *News Group Newspapers Limited* [1997] FSR 600, Jacob J followed the same principle in a case in which a newspaper sought to publish information about features of an intimate homosexual relationship.

Outside the domestic area of life, the courts have, for example, restrained publication of photographs in circumstances in which the photographers would have known that the occasion was a private one and the taking of photographs by outsiders was not permitted (see, for example, *Creation Records Ltd* v *Newsgroup Newspapers Ltd* [1997] EMLR 444 and *Shelley Films Ltd* v *Rex Features Ltd* [1994] EMLR 134).

So, also, in *A* v *United Kingdom* 27 EHRR 611, English law was held not to be in breach of the Convention in a case involving publication of pictures of Lady Spencer in a private clinic taken with a tele-photo lens under English law.

However, despite the development of the law of confidentiality and incidentally, the law with regard to breach of fiduciary duties and publication of official secrets (particularly abroad), until recently the law categorically denied that there was any tort of privacy (see *Kaye* v *Robertson* [1991] FSR 62.

Academics and some extra judicial commentaries over the last ten years have suggested that an extension of the action for breach of confidence could fill the gap in English law which is filled by privacy law in many other countries.

However, the incorporation of the European Convention of Human Rights into English law and in particular article 8, the right to privacy, has meant that the law in this area will need to be reviewed. An indication of a potential change in judicial attitudes may be seen by the recent case of *Douglas and Zeta-Jones and Northern and Shell PLC v Hello! Ltd* (2000) LTL 21 December. In substance the Court of Appeal refused to grant an injunction restraining *Hello!* Magazine for publishing photographs of Michael Douglas and Catherine Zeta-Jones' wedding even though the couple had already sold the rights to OK! Magazine.

The court held that there was clearly a serious triable issue as to whether the photographs had been taken at a private function, such as to be subject to rights of privacy and confidentiality. Further, English law recognised the right to privacy in accordance with Article 8 European Convention on Human Rights. However, it was clear from the jurisprudence of the European Court of Human Rights that there were different degrees of privacy, and that those different degrees materially affected the interaction between the right to privacy and the right to freedom of expression conferred by Article 12 of the Convention.

In the instant case the wedding was far from being a private one. The major part of the couple's privacy rights had been sold as part of a commercial transaction. In the instant case the balance of convenience militated against the grant of an injunction. On the one hand, any damage sustained by the third claimant was capable of being quantified by requiring an account of the profits made by the defendant in respect of the allegedly infringing issue of *Hello!* magazine. On the other hand, if publication of the issue of *Hello!* magazine was "killed", the defendant would suffer loss which it would be extremely difficult to quantify.

The comments made by the court led to Frances Gibb in *The Times* (on 22 December 2000) heralding the judgment as "New privacy right won by Zeta-Jones" and claiming that "A new right of privacy in English law was created".

Lord Justice Sedley said that the law had to protect those "who find themselves subjected to an unwarranted intrusion into lives". He added, "Mr Douglas and Miss Zeta-Jones have a powerful prima facie claim to redress for invasion of their privacy as a qualified right recognised and protected by English law."

The judges also made clear that even where celebrities struck deals to publicise themselves, they could claim privacy over those deals.

Mr Douglas and Miss Zeta-Jones could claim such a privacy right even though the major part of their privacy rights "have become the subject of a commercial transaction," he said. "Bluntly, they have been sold." But the couple had retained privacy in the shape of editorial control over *OK!*'s pictures. "They were careful by their contract to retain a right of veto over publication of *OK!*'s photographs in order to maintain the kind of image which is professionally and no doubt also personally important to them. This element of privacy remained theirs and *Hello!*'s photographs no doubt violated it."

In the light of this decision and the incorporation of the Convention into English law it remains to be seen how the law will develop in this area.

What is clear is that caution should be the keyword when consideration is given to forwarding an e-mail which potentially may contain confidential or private information.

In any event, the practical effects of such disclosure may sometimes be even worse that the legal ones. This was most recently seen in December 2000 when a lawyer forwarded a private e-mail from his girl friend about a sex act. Within hours gossip about the girlfriend's enjoyment of the act had been cir-culated to millions of internet users from America to Japan and even Australia. The lawyer and five others at his firm were disciplined but not dis-missed. In addition, nine staff were suspended by the Financial Services Authority for forwarding the sexually explicit e-mail through the regulator's computer system (see *The Times*, 15 December 2000, 18 December 2000, 20 December 2000 and 22 December 2000).

CHAPTER 7
NEGLIGENCE

INTRODUCTION

The tort of negligence has an extremely wide ambit. It covers matters such as an auditor's negligent misstatement resulting in financial loss on the international scale, through to simple road traffic accidents. This chapter aims to address the key areas of negligence which are likely to be of significance for e-mail users.

Negligence is by definition a wide tort which can affect e-mail users in differing ways. For instance, a lawyer offering an on-line advice service must consider the position if the advice given is incorrect or negligent. It could amount to a negligent misstatement which could lead to liability. What happens if the person receiving the advice forwards it on to another party in a similar position? Is that other person enabled by that to sue on the strength of the advice? As a by product of all of this and more it will be prudent for all users to consider their insurance cover.

THE CONSTITUENT PARTS OF NEGLIGENCE

In order to succeed in a claim for negligence, four factors must be shown:

1. the existence of a duty of care (i.e. that the third party owed some duty in law to take care against committing the act which has created the damage);

2. a breach of that duty of care by the third party (i.e. failing to take reasonable care);

3. a causal connection between the third party's carelessness and the damage which resulted;

4. that it has caused foreseeable damage.

In some ways foreseeability seeps into each of the above. For instance, the more likely or foreseeable something is to happen, then the more likelihood that there will be a duty imposed. The more foreseeable that harm is to occur, then when it does occur, the more likely it is that the Defendant acted carelessly and without regard to the likely consequences. Finally, the type of harm and the individual so harmed must be foreseeable in order to recover. This has, in no small part, policy considerations. Further the implications for e-mail and the internet are obviously important.

Duty of Care

The categories are not restricted in relation to (1), above, and the tort is flexibly applied according to the satisfaction of the courts that there exists a certain proximity between the claimant and defendant and such a duty is in the public interest. It was as long ago as 1932 when the "neighbour principle" was first truly crystallised (see *Donoghue* v *Stevenson* [1932] A.C. 562). Essentially a court is looking to see whether the person who has suffered the damage should have been considered by the person committing the tort before doing what he did. In this sense it is another factor in defining the duty to prevent harm and the extent of the same:

> "…in addition to the foreseeability of damage, necessary ingredients in any situation giving rise to a duty of care are that there should exist between the party owing the duty and the person to whom it is owed a relationship characterised by the law as one of "proximity" or "neighbourhood" and that the situation should be one in which the court considers it fair, just and reasonable that the law should impose a duty of a given scope on the one party for the benefit of the other"

> (per Lord Bridge, *Caparo Industries plc* v *Dickman* [1990] 2 A.C. 605 at 617–618).

This test may need careful consideration now that the internet has opened communication links hitherto restricted.

The damage must be foreseeable and proximate. This means that the court will look at the person concerned and consider what knowledge he *should* have had and then look at the harm concerned. The greater the awareness of harm, then the greater duty to take care to prevent it from occurring. In determining proximity the courts will look at physical proximity (in the sense of speed and time) between the parties, circumstantial proximity such as an overriding relationship (e.g. of professional relationship such as solicitor and client) and causal proximity (i.e. "closeness or directness of the causal connection or relationship between the particular course of conduct and the loss or injury sustained", per Deane J. *Sunderland Shire Council* v *Heyman* (1985) 60 A.L.R. 1 at 55 – 56). The latter may be established where for instance there is a voluntary assumption of responsibility (see below).

It is suggested therefore that there are no closed categories and that in relation to internet matters the courts will be looking for some directness between the parties concerned. In addition they will weigh up the balance: on the one hand there needs to be compensation for wrongs and on the other that legal responsibility should not become to burdensome comply with. This will involve consideration not just of the individual factual circumstances but also the movement of social and economic forces which may have altered stances on public policy. This was much the case when in 1995 it was held that there was a duty on an employer in giving a reference (*Spring* v *Guardian Assurance plc* [1995] 2 A.C. 296). Their Lordships took into account the increasing openness in employment relationships and that therefore it was reasonable and just to impose a duty. This will obviously apply to all employment references sent by e-mail (though also see *Kidd* v *AXA Equity & Law Life Assurance Society plc and anor* [2000] IRLR 301). Importantly it shows that the courts will be looking at what is socially expected as well as technical legal rules. More than anything it demonstrates the flexibility of the tort. The courts will also put into the balance the wider picture. For instance, would a successful claim lead to the "floodgates" being opened to masses of litigation?

The duty of care may not be as wide as otherwise would be the case if there exists a contractual provision so as to exclude liability and limiting the duty. The provision would not take any contractual effect with other parties but it may affect the factors leading to a duty.

One example of interest is to be found in the decision of the Court of Appeal in *A E Beckett & Sons (Lyndons) Limited and others v Midland Electricity plc* (CA, unrep, Times LR 10/1/01) (this is subject to a possible appeal). There an electricity company sought to exclude liability for economic loss by relying on a widely drafted disclaimer. Of great importance was the meaning to ascribe to section 21 Electricity Act 1989. The Court looked at the parliamentary debate on the subject and concluded that section 21(b) was to meet the concerns regarding the possible liability which might flow from interruption of supply to computers in major corporates. The section was designed, therefore, to allow exclusion of liability for the consequences of effect upon the supply of electricity.

There is generally no duty of care for pure economic loss. Pure economic loss is that which has no connection with any physical damage to person or property. It is generally that seen as loss associated with negligent advice or reliance on negligent statements. The rule is explained by considering that "whilst the links between negligence and physical damage depend largely on the laws of nature and necessarily limit the type of relationship giving rise to a claim, those between negligence and pure economic loss are primarily human in creation and can form a complex web through which economic losses can ripple out from the one negligent act. Secondly, because the economic relationships are frequently created rather than imposed, the participants in the web have a greater opportunity to use contracts to determine the level of risk to be taken" (see *Clerk & Lindsell on Torts*, 18th ed. 7–85). There is no general duty even when foreseeable: see *Hamble Fisheries Limited v L Gardner & Sons Limited* [1999] 2 Lloyd's Rep 1.

EXAMPLE

Venture-Capitalist guru Valerio Massimo hires PR king Tom Hampson to handle his business' media relations. Whilst Valerio Massimo is in negotiations with club tycoon James Rocelli to buy a controlling share in his entertainment empire Sak PLC, business journalist Simon Nixon arranges to interview Valerio Massimo. Valerio Massimo seeks advice from Tom Hampson by e-mail. He uses the address advertised on Tom Hampson's letterhead. Unfortunately, Tom Hampson is on holiday in the South of France and does not collect his e-mail. Valerio Massimo's interview goes very badly and he suffers damage.

Did Tom Hampson owe Valerio Massimo a duty of care to regularly check his e-mails?

The rule is not restricted to loss of profits from business but also financial losses of individuals: see *Greenfield v Dr Irwin, Dr Cullen, Dr Flatter* (CA, unrep, 24/1/01, LTL 24/1/01); *McFarlane and anor v Tayside Health Board* [1999] 3 WLR 1301; but also see *Nunnerley and anor v Warrington HA and anor* [2000] Lloyd's Rep Med 170.

E-mail is in some ways a secretive form of communication. The mail goes directly on to the user's own system, and may be password protected. It lacks that tangible quality which exists in other forms of communication (for instance a telephone call will usually go to somebody who can advise you on their position, a fax comes through to the office to be seen by others, letters are received as a documents and so on). Voicemail also may suffer the same problems as e-mail but this can be mitigated by the voicemail owner leaving his or her whereabouts on the recorded message.

With mail boxes, e-mails can simply sit unopened until they are activated. Companies may need to think carefully about supervision of employees' e-mails when they go away on holiday, transfer or leave the company. There must be in place an effective retrieval system. This can be achieved either by technical means (e.g. mail diversion) or by company policy in that individuals would be responsible for the supervision of e-mail accounts when colleagues are away from their desk. It may also be dealt with by a standard e-mail response advising the sender the whereabouts of the intended recipient and what will now happen with the mail. In any event, the issues of privacy and fair and adequate supervision must be considered. These are dealt with in other parts of this work.

Negligent Misstatement

Makers of negligent statements can find themselves responsible for economic loss if certain criteria are fulfilled. The lead case in the area is *Hedly Byrne & Co Ltd* v *Heller & Partners Ltd* [1964] A.C. 465. Therein it was held that where there was no disclaimer or other matter restricting the duty of care, it was possible for there to exist a duty of care when a party makes a negligent statement where it was to be relied upon by others, who did in fact rely upon it, and who suffered loss as a result. It is also now clear that the ratio in *Hedly Byrne* applies to all economic losses caused by negligence and not just that caused by a negligent misstatement. The test has been subject to review and comment since its being stated and there seemingly exists more than one way to explain the requirements to satisfy the test. It would appear, at least, that it must be shown that a negligent statement has been made, that it was made to someone for which the maker assumed some responsibility, that the statement was relied upon and that loss followed. In determining the same the courts will be mindful of public policy and other factors similar to those mentioned above.

Reliance on the statement must be shown. Thus it must be shown that it was actually relied upon in fact and secondly that it was reasonable to so rely. Imagine that friends, both surveyors and both having inspected a property, e-mailed one another about a property being good value at its market price. One of the surveyors purchases the property. The property turns out to be hiding an inherent defect. Both surveyors were negligent to miss the defect. It would be a requirement that the purchasing surveyor relied on the e-mails as sent by the friend. The claim would probably falter due firstly to the fact of his being a surveyor himself and thereby would not have relied on the advice (if it can be so properly called) contained within the e-mails, and secondly that it was not reasonable to impose a duty of responsibility where there was no special relationship of trust and reliance. The latter would be different were the advice given by an expert to a customer (aside from contractual rights) or where there is a general expectation of reliance (for instance the preparation of wills by solicitors: see *White* v *Jones* [1995] 2 AC 207 "Although in any particular case it may not be possible to demonstrate that the intended beneficiary relied upon the solicitor, society as a whole does rely on solicitors to carry out their will making functions carefully" (per Lord Browne Wilkinson at page 276 B-C).

Further, it is important to have Lord Browne Wilkinson's words in mind when dealing with reliance: "in the case of a duty of care flowing from a fiduciary relationship liability is not dependent upon actual reliance by the plaintiff on the defendant's actions but on the fact that, as the fiduciary is well aware, the plaintiff's economic well being is dependent upon the proper discharge by the fiduciary of his duty" (at 275 G).

Six factors of importance in considering whether to impose a duty were identified by Neill LJ in *James McNaughton Paper Group Ltd* v *Hicks Anderson & Co* [1991] 2 QB 113:

1. the purpose for which the statement was made;

2. the purpose for which the statement was communicated;

3. the relationship between the adviser, the person receiving the advice and any other party involved;

4. the size or number of any class which the person receiving the information belongs;

5. the state of knowledge of the adviser;

6. reliance by the advisor.

Similar factors were also referred to in *Bank of Credit & Commerce International (Overseas) Limited (In Liquidation) and others* v *(1) Price Waterhouse and others, (2) Ernst & Whinney & others* [1998] BCC 617 where it was also stated that the absence of others to rely upon may also be relevant along with the opportunity, or otherwise, given to add a disclaimer.

The **purpose for which the statement was made** is important as it obviously indicates the context of duty between the parties. For instance in the example above, the e-mails between the two friends were obviously as friends as opposed to adviser and advisee. In *Caparo* (supra.) the audit report was relied upon by shareholders in making investment decisions. The House of Lords held that the purpose of an audit report, in its statutory sense, was to enable shareholders to exercise their proprietary interests in the management of the company and did not extend to making investment decisions.

Where, however, the context is slightly different a duty may well arise. Such a duty was evident in *The Law Society* v *KPMG Peat Marwick* [2000] WLR 1991; Lloyd's Rep. PN 219, where it was held that a duty existed where accountants were instructed by solicitors to report on their accounts as the purpose of the same was to assist the Law Society in supervision of compliance with the accounting rules. In determining the purpose of the document the court will take into account any statutory reasons, any contractual provisions and the surrounding events related to the provision of the information.

For example in *White* v *Jones* (supra.) it was commented that the statement was made as part of the solicitor's duty in drafting the will. The beneficiary was wholly dependent upon the solicitor exercising due care and skill in doing so. The creation of the will was the very purpose of the statement.

The **purpose for which the statement was communicated** can assist in the determination of duty. Thus a statement made for one purpose to X may be relied upon by Y. It may not be appropriate to do so in these circumstances and therefore the actual facts must be looked at closely. In *Smith* v *Eric S. Bush* [1990] 1 A.C. 831 a surveyor's report prepared for a building society (in order to achieve compliance with statutory provisions regulating loans) was relied upon by the purchaser of the property concerned as to its valuation. The House of Lords held that a duty existed. In doing so they stressed two factors: first that the surveyors knew that the prospective purchaser would probably rely on it and that second the prospective purchaser had paid the building society a fee to defray the surveyor's fee. These factors along with the whole picture meant that the surveyor had assumed a responsibility to the prospective purchaser.

The **relationship between the adviser, the person receiving the advice and any other party involved** is a matter of fact and degree more than anything else. The cases of *Caparo* and *Eric S. Bush* (supra.) are good factual examples of the operation of this area. Essentially the court will look to see whether the person relying upon the statement has any direct or other reasonable nexus with the statement maker in order to determine the scope of the duty. This will include any agreements between the parties which may appear inconsistent with an assumption of responsibility.

In *Henderson* v *Merrett Syndicates Ltd* [1995] 2 AC 145 the defendant assumed to act in the claimant's affair pursuant to a contract with a third party. This was held not to be necessarily incompatible with the finding that the defendant had also entered into a special relationship with the claimant, despite the lack of contact between the two.

Some relationships, by definition, include a duty to one another. A classic example is employer and employee (for instance to provide a safe place of work). However, when considering advice and assistance there may be instances where no duty exists. In *Outram* v *Academy Plastics* [2000] IRLR 499 it was held that there was no duty in tort to advise employees as to the benefits and operation of the pension scheme. This may not necessarily be the case were there a contractual basis for such an argument. The Court held that it was not reasonable to expect the company to give pensions advice, a very complex subject, to employees.

The **size or number of any class which the person receiving the information belongs** is relevant and goes to the extent of the potential liability. Courts will be slow to create a duty where the existence of the same would create a large amount of potential claims. The particularly unsatisfactory aspect to such a duty existing is, arguably, not the number of the potential claimants but instead the indeterminacy of the same (see the judgment of McHugh J. in *Perre* v *Apand Pty Ltd* [1999] A.L.R. 606 at 633). It is suggested that where the possible claimants are not identifiable then there must exist some other counterbalance such as being members of a determinate class of people in order for a duty to exist: see *Clerk & Lindsell On Torts,* 18th ed. 7–110 and *Preston* v *Torfaen B.C.* (1993) 36 Con LR 48. This is an important area for development in the internet field.

The duty will be limited to "transactions or types of transactions of which the **adviser had knowledge** and will only arise where the adviser knows or ought to know that the [advice] will be relied on by a particular person or class of persons in connection with that transaction" (per Neill LJ *McNaughton* supra.). It does not matter that the adviser did not intend for his advice to be relied upon as indeed it transpired to be. It is also relevant to consider whether the adviser knew that the advisee would not seek any independent or other advice. If it could be assumed that they would do so, then it is more likely to point away from the imposition of a duty.

A case dealing with such an issue is *Fashion Brokers Limited* v *Clarke Hayes (a firm) and Cannock Chase Council* (2000) PNLR 473. The Court of Appeal, in refusing to impose liability for an alleged misstatement, found that the shortness of the telephone call and the failure to identify who was providing the information led to the conclusion that it was not reasonable for the information to be relied upon.

With e-mail the communication is less formal than perhaps a letter, however, arguably more so than than a telephone call (given its potentially permanent form). Communications by e-mail may, therefore, be seen as a clearer indication that there is reliance. For instance, if a client were to say to his professional adviser over the telephone "could you please send me an e-mail recording what you have just told me", this may suggest that the client intends to rely on the advice in some way. This may, therefore, elevate the significance of the initial discussion.

We have already seen that there must be reasonable reliance by the advisee. This includes an assessment of whether the person was entitled to treat the advice as final or whether it should be checked. If there is no reliance in fact or no reasonable reliance permitted, then there can be no duty irrespective of the other areas referred to above. The question can only be answered on the facts of each individual case. In *McNaughton* Neill considered the position in relation to business transactions conducted at arms' length (at 126) and commented as follows:

"...in business transactions conducted at arms' length it may sometimes be difficult for an advisee to prove that he was entitled to act on a statement without taking any independent advice..."

This will be a consoling thought for all e-businesses which arguably provide "advice" and assistance in matters such as the purchase of shares. The flip side of the coin is that with so much information and assistance available over the internet, it may be increasingly implicit that other advice or assistance is sought and that the reliance upon one source is consequently diminished in the eyes of the court.

Where the advice is given either outside the sphere of one's profession or in a social context, it is unlikely to attract legal responsibility. There is, however, no rule to this effect and the contrary may be shown to exist. E-mail users are cautioned to use care in the drafting and content of e-mails. For these reasons matters such as "sales talk" will not generally attract a duty of care (see e.g. *Shields* v *Broderick* [1984] 8 D.L.R. (4th) 96). In the assessment of reasonable reliance it may be reasonable to rely upon a corporate for particular work, but not reasonable to rely upon the corporate's employee undertaking the work. Whilst appearing anomalous, this is based upon the fact that the recipient "could not reasonably rely for indemnification on the individual engineers" (see *Edgeworth Constructions Ltd* v *N.D. Lea & Associates Ltd* [1993] 107 D.L.R. (4th) 169).

The infamous case of *Hedley Byrne* was resolved in favour of the advisor as there was a disclaimer. The effect of the disclaimer was that it prevented the duty of care from arising. It is not therefore comparable to an exclusion clause, but instead is an important factor in the material for the court to consider when assessing whether the imposition of a duty is reasonable. The disclaimer must be sufficient to cover the conduct in question. Disclaimers will, as other terms, be subject to regulation by the Unfair Contract Terms Act 1977, which is dealt with elsewhere in this work and not repeated herein.

Breach of Duty

In order to breach the duty in law there has to be a failure to exercise reasonable care and skill. The important factor to appreciate is that this is an objective assessment. There is an element of subjectivity at the outset of this investigation. Members of professions will be judged by the acceptable and reasonable standards expected of that profession. The majority of the leading cases in this field have been medically orientated. They are expected to exercise the ordinary skill of a competent man exercising that particular art (see *Bolam* v *Friern Hospital Management Committee* [1957] 1 WLR 582) which may differ with their speciality or the post which they hold (see *Maynard* v *West Midlands Regional Health Authority* [1984] 1 WLR 634 and *Wilsher* v *Essex Area Health Authority* [1988] AC 174).

EXAMPLE

Don Laurenzo di Firenze receives an e-mail with the heading "I LOVE YOU" from his wife Elizabeth Renzoni-Dick. It is well known in Italy, where he lives, that a new love bug is doing the rounds. It consists of an e-mail entitled "I LOVE YOU" and when opened forwards itself to all those in the recipient's address book and then deletes the hard disc. Despite this, Don Laurenzo opens the e-mail. Unfortunately, it is the love bug and it immediately forwards itself to all those in his address book, including champion golfer Richard Hall who lives on Saltspring Island off Canada where news of the love bug has not yet been reported. Richard Hall opens the e-mail and as well as the bug being forwarded, it also deletes his hard disc causing him damage.

Does Don Laurenzo owe Richard Hall a duty of care?

If so, does he breach that duty by opening the e-mail?

The assessment of whether a breach of duty has taken place will obviously include consideration of any applicable professional guidance, whether that be mandatory within the profession or not.

Foreseeable Damage

It is also necessary to show both that some damage to the claimant was fore-seeable and also that the nature of that damage was foreseeable. Firstly, the claimant first, therefore must be owed a duty (see above) and secondly the kind of harm must be foreseeable. In *Ward* v *Cannock Chase District Council* [1986] Ch. 546 the defendant owned a neighbouring terraced house to the claimant. The defendant moved the claimant out of the his own property and allowed the neighbouring property to go derelict, in turn causing damage to the claimant's house. Vandals subsequently broke into the derelict house and stole some articles belonging to the claimant. It was held that a duty existed to the claimant and that (1) the damage to the house was foreseeable and they were answerable for it; but that (2) there was no liability for the stolen articles as it was not foreseeable that the claimant would not have removed the arti-cles before the theft.

Once breach of duty has been established, the level of foreseeability required is slight. *Clerk & Lindsell on Torts*, summarise the leading cases in this field as follows: "as long as some damage, however slight, of a particular kind was foreseeable to the person or property of the claimant, he can recover for the full extent of it though neither the extent nor precise manner of its incidence was foreseeable" (Eighteenth edition, 7–142, commenting upon *The Wagon Mound* case law [1961] A.C. 388; [1967] 1 A.C. 617).

In *Banque Bruxelles* v *Eagle Star Ins.* [1996] 3 WLR 87 the House of Lords considered foreseeable loss and concluded that where a person who is under a duty to take reasonable care to provide information on which someone else would decide on a particular course of action, and where that duty was breached, then the liability would be for the foreseeable loss flowing from the information being wrong, and not for the entirety of the actual loss which occurred. This obviously recognises the differing rule of recovery for tort and contract: "the tort measure is the extent to which the plaintiff is worse off because the information is wrong whereas the warranty measure is the extent to which he would have been better off if the information had been right" (per Lord Hoffmann at 97F).

"Kind of damage" should not be narrowly construed, especially in relation to personal injury matters (see *Hughes* v *Lord Advocate* [1963] A.C. 837). Further, it is the general law that the tortfeasor must take their victim as they find them (i.e. the claimant suffered increased harm or damage due to a peculiar susceptibility. The defendant is still answerable if it be shown that he breached a duty owed to the claimant).

NUISANCE

Nuisance is concerned with activity which unduly interferes with another's use or enjoyment of land. Public nuisance is unlikely to be of relevance to this work and is not considered herein. Nuisance is concerned with indirect entry on to another's land. Direct entry is covered by trespass. Therefore a computer hacker may be viewed as a trespasser and not a nuisance. Interference from a mobile telephone attached to a laptop which affects the television reception next door, however, could well be a nuisance rather than a trespass (see *Clerk & Lindsell*, 18th ed., paragraph 19–13 and the cases cited therein). The difference lies, not least, in the fact that for nuisance the claimant must prove special damage before an action will succeed.

RYLANDS V FLETCHER LIABILITY

This area of law is named after the case which established it. The nature of the tort is strict liability. Once its constituent parts are made out, there is no obligation to prove negligence. The classic definition was given by Blackburn J.: "...the person who for his own purposes brings on his lands and collects and keeps there anything likely to do mischief if it escapes must keep it in at his peril, and, if he does not do so, is prima facie answerable for all the damage which is the natural consequence of its escape" (see (1866) L.R. 1 Ex 265 at page 279). The decision was affirmed in the House of Lords (see (1886) L.R. 3 HL 330, HL) where the necessity for the material so kept to be a non-natural use of the land, was added.

The nature and scope of the doctrine has undergone judicial erosion since its declaration. In the most recent case in the House of Lords, it was held that "it is more appropriate for strict liability in respect of operations of high risk to be imposed by Parliament…" (per Lord Goff: *Cambridge Water Company Ltd* v *Eastern Counties Leather plc* [1994] 2 A.C. 264 at 305. The free standing concept of the tort has been held in Australia to no longer exist and instead simply part of negligence (see *Burnie Part Authority* v *General Jones Pty Ltd* (1994) 120 A.L.R. 42).

The key constituent parts are as follows:

(1) That the use of the land is non-natural; and,

(2) That the thing stored or collected there for his own purposes is likely to do mischief if it escapes (NOT that is likely to escape, as this is not a necessary constituent); and,

(3) There is natural damage caused.

The tort has a tentative application to computer viruses or other material obtained from the internet or e-mail system. For example, a computer programmer is in the process of writing anti virus software. In order to undertake his work he tests several of the current viruses out on the system. Whilst doing so the virus is unwittingly, and unforeseeably, transmitted to other computer users causing damage to financial details and leading to computer engineer's bills and economic loss of profits. Is he responsible? The court would have to satisfy itself of the factors listed above. It is suggested that computer programming would be seen as a natural use of the land. As a result the action would falter. However, such a proposition is not tested by authority and the cases dealing with whether the use of the land is natural or not, are concerned, unsurprisingly, with matters relating to more tangible uses of the land. It should be noted that the restriction against claims for purely economic loss applies in this tort as with negligence (see above).

Viruses unwittingly held by companies and unwittingly sent will not, it is suggested, incur any potential liability as the viruses were not brought on to the land for the company's "own purposes".

Assuming that the test was satisfied the next question is whether the thing is dangerous or likely to cause mischief. In this regard and the destructive nature of computer viruses it is suggested that if the tort were allowed to expand and not to be restrictively construed, viruses would be so defined. The closest, though still very much removed, example which has been held to be dangerous and covered under the tort is electricity.

The liability is potentially owed to all those affected. The application of such a principle would certainly need careful consideration in the limits of its liability. A similar curtailment of responsibility may be exercised as was in the nuisance case of *Hunter* v *Canary Wharf Ltd* [1997] A.C. 655 whereby it was held that a claimant had to have an interest in land in order to pursue the claim. Liability will be restricted to damage which is foreseeable: see *Cambridge Water* at 306, and above.

The exceptions to the rule are as follows. Where there is:

(i) an act of God;

(ii) an act or default of the claimant;

(iii) the consent of the claimant;

(iv) the independent act of a third party; or

(v) authorisation by statute, etc.

The most important of these in the current context is act of a third party. There will be no liability if the thing has escaped by the independent act of a third party where the defendant has not been negligent. Where the act of a third party is not intentional but instead negligent, then liability may still exist as there is a duty for those with dangerous things to guard against negligence of others. Whether or not necessity can amount to a defence is, it appears, open at present: see *Rigby* v *Chief Constable of Northamptonshire* [1985] 2 All E.R. 985.

It is suggested that given the erosion of the tort, it is unlikely to affect this area of law. However, it is yet another area which must be considered by all those concerned.

CHAPTER 8
INTELLECTUAL PROPERTY

INTRODUCTION

Information is intangible and yet can have a great deal more value than any fixed, solid object or chattel. As a result the law has long recognised the need to protect such information from unwarranted users. The law of intellectual property aims to protect ideas, knowledge, innovation and information. With the internet making transmission, copying and dissemination of information very much easier, it is not difficult to appreciate why this area of law will be significantly affected.

The most important parts of the law of intellectual property are:

    (a) copyright;

    (b) trade marks;

    (c) passing off;

    (d) patents; and

    (e) design rights.

The wealth of law on these topics is easily appreciable by reference to the leading texts, this chapter merely gives an overview of the general law and then goes into more detail with the applicability of the same in relation to e-mail and the internet.

COPYRIGHT

Copying computer products and information is an easy and commonplace thing to do. The value of the products and information must, therefore, be protected by some mechanism. Copyright aims to protect such information from unlawful appropriation and repetition. Copyright is not subject to registration (unlike Trade Marks and Patents), and therefore is created as and when the product / information is created.

The nature of copyright is to prohibit the exploitation or ones work without permission. The work must have included some exertion of skill and labour. The nature of the right is not based on the end product and the similarity thereto, but instead upon the actual use of the skill and labour in creating the work.

Work attracting copyright

The following attract the protection of copyright:

(a) original literary, dramatic, musical or artistic works;

(b) sound recordings, films, broadcasts or cable programmes; and

(c) the typographical arrangement of published editions.

(see section 1(1) *Copyright, Designs and Patents Act 1988*)

The requirement for "originality" for the first items listed above is not so required for those listed under (b) and (c) above. However, that is not to say that the work will be protected if, in itself, it is a mere copy. Originality requires the expending of some skill and effort: see *Ladbroke (Football) Ltd* v *William Hill (Football) Ltd* [1964] 1 WLR 273, though the level of the same is not particularly difficult to establish. Originality can be shown despite the work being based upon other works. The real question is the existence of skill and effort. A collage of pictures will, therefore, be an original work despite being made up of various existing works. It will therefore attract copyright (even if in some parts it may be infringing others' copyright).

There are two requirements to attract protection: firstly that the work is produced by a qualified person and secondly that for artistic, literary, musical or dramatic works the work must be recorded in some form. The first is satisfied if the author is a British citizen (or of a similar status) or a body corporate incorporated in the UK (or where the Act applies): see Chapter IX of the Act.

The second requirement is satisfied by recording it in writing or otherwise. For instance a song may be written down by hand or typed into an e-mail. Writing is defined as including any "form of notation or code, whether by hand or otherwise and regardless of the method by which or medium in or on which it is recorded" (section 178). Therefore it is suggested that e-mail can attract copyright protection.

In relation to the computer industry and the services provided over the internet, the amount and types of copyright are mind boggling. Seemingly simple computer images may attract multifarious copyrights. For instance in the musical composition, the graphics images, the programming language, and any text appearing on the screen are but a few of the more obvious copyrights. Photographs, which expended skill and effort, attracted copyright protection in *Antiquesportfolio.com plc* v *Rodney Fitch & Co Ltd* (2000) IPD November 23092, Times LR 21 July 2000, LTL 10/7/2000 (Ch. D, Neuberger J.).

Databases will attract copyright subject to their being original in their selection or arrangement (see section 3A(2), as inserted by the Copyright and Rights in Databases Regulations 1997 (SI 1997/3032).

Web-sites will probably attract copyright in themselves (given the time, effort and creativity expended) and as a database under the 1997 Regulations (incorporating the Database Directive 1996). The Database right is essentially recognising the time and effort which can be spent organising a database and giving some protection for the same. It is an important right for businesses who seek to restrain ex-employees on the use of such information without the need for them to show that there has been a specific breach of confidentiality. In order to attract protection it need be shown that the database was organised in a systematic or methodical way, the system or method need not, as with copyright, be an intellectual creation. The duration of such protection is 15 years from its making.

The mere assistance of a computer in creating work is not such so as to reduce the originality: see *Express Newspapers plc* v *Liverpool Daily Post & Echo plc* [1985] 1 WLR 1089.

The Protection of Copyright

Copyright will be breached if anyone, without permission:

- copies the work;
- issues copies to the public
- performs, plays or shows the work in public;
- rents or lends the work to the public;
- broadcasting the work or including it in a cable programme;
- adapts the work.

Anyone authorising any of the above will also become an infringer (section 16(2)). It is suggested that "authorisation" implies some kind of approval, encouragement or control and does not suggest merely providing the access to the material (as ISPs inevitably do). This would be consistent with previous authority which held public libraries and such other renting / lending bodies, or those providing facilities for copying, as not authorising infringement: see

CBS Songs Ltd v *Amstrad Consumer Electronics plc* [1988] AC 1013; *CBS Inc.* v *Ames Records and Tapes Ltd* [1982] Ch. 91.

It should be noted however, that the test is a factual one and will depend upon the circumstances of each case. A US example of a finding of authorisation can be seen in the cases involving Sega (*Sega Enterprises* v *Sabella* and *Sega Enterprises* v *Maphia* US District Court for the District of Northern California, 18 December 1995, 16 December 1996, respectively). Sega were held to have authorised the breach of copyright due to the amount of assistance that the particular company gave to those who were likely to infringe such rights.

It is likely that ISPs will remain protected so long as they have acted reasonably in preventing such infringement once it is apparent to them (much like in *Godfrey* v *Demon* – see chapter on defamation). Such an approach is reflected in legislation in the USA which exempts liability where there is little or no blame to be placed at the feet of the service provider: see the Digital Millennium Copyright Act 1998, see also the EU Directive 2000/31/EC. This area is one that is sure to develop with speed.

It will be a breach of copyright to store the works by electronic means (section 17(2)). It will be a breach of copyright if the act is in relation to the whole or a substantial part of the work (see section 16(3)). "Substantial" copying could be shown where an identifiable part of the whole had been copied (as in *Ladbroke (Football) Ltd* v *William Hill (Football) Ltd* [1964] 1 WLR 273) or where the copying had been with modifications ("altered copying"). In the case of altered copying the Court will find it helpful to assess whether the infringer incorporated a substantial part of the independent skill, labour and other matters contributed by the original author in creating the work (see Laddie, Prescott and Vitoria, *The Modern Law of Copyright and Designs* (1995, 2nd edition). The test is therefore recognising the very bedrock of copyright law: i.e. that it is the skill and effort which should be protected. Similarities in the work will often be determinative as to the issue of copying and the substantiality of any such copying: see the recent case of *Designer Guild Limited* v *Russell Williams (Textiles) Limited (t/a Washington DC)* [2000] 1 WLR 2416.

Web-sites can amount to cable programmes and therefore fall into the broadcasting provision outlined above: see *Shetland Times* v *Wills* [1997] FSR 604; [1997] EMLR 277.

Ownership and duration of copyright

The owner is prima facie the author of the work. This is subject to exceptions, the most obvious being where an employee creates a work in the course of his employment (not self employment). There, the copyright lies with the employer (see section 11(2)). Copyright can also be assigned or transferred.

Copyright will persist for varying periods depending on the type of work. Generally, the periods are as follows. For literary, dramatic, musical or artistic works: 70 years from death of the author. For films: 70 years from the death of the principal director and author (whichever is later). For publication of a previously unpublished work whose period of protection has lapsed (the "publication right"): 25 years from publication. For a computer generated work: 50 years from the end of the year when the work was made. Typographical arrangement of a published edition: 25 years from the end of the year when first published.

In *Shetland Times* v *Wills* [1997] FSR 604; [1997] EMLR 277 the *Shetland Times* were the creators and owners of the *Shetland Times* news web site. Readers could access the site's front page and the click on to the headlines to see the full text of any particular story. A rival web site displayed the headlines of the *Shetland Times* with the capability to enter the stories without going via the front page of the *Shetland Times'* web site. The *Shetland Times* brought an action for breach of copyright and were granted interim restraint. The *Shetland Times* were hoping to sell advertising space on the home page and the direct link to cut out the home page was obviously potentially detrimental. The case settled before the final hearing with a compromise about the use of the headlines so as to allow the origin to be clearly marked.

MP3: the copyright struggle

Perhaps the most important and hotly contested copyright issue to hit cyberspace is the dispute between the music industry, broadcasters and internet facility providers. The technology is such that the compression of CD quality sound and the transmission of such sound, can be done in a matter of minutes.

A crude definition of compression is the process by which analogue sound (i.e. that used by CDs and tapes) is transferred into a digital format. The process is highly technical and irrelevant for this work, however, it is important to note that the process used to be slow and cumbersome, whereas of late this process has speeded up dramatically.

The progress seriously threatens the copyright holders' ability to control public performance, broadcast, reproduction and distribution. The CDs which have been released to current day have lacked any electronic limitations to reproduction. Therefore reproduction on a mass scale without any loss of quality is possible.

The law must move on to reflect such changes. Various amendments may be considered to the Copyright, Designs and Patents Act 1988 to prohibit the sale of machinery which removes security tags or other devices to limit repro-duction. As yet, nothing has been done which is likely to stem the inevitable flow of piracy. The industry themselves may seek protection by selling music online which has to be decrypted. The sites would have to be competitive to lure customers away from the temptation of piracy. The use of existing links with distribution outlets (who are now predominantly on-line) may facilitate in accessing a pre-existing client base who are already transacting with credit cards over the internet. In this vein digital music is sold as would be a CD.

Whatever strategy is adopted by the major music companies, it will have to be secure, reliable, efficient and economic. Otherwise, piracy will simply be too attractive an alternative to ignore for those internet users whom put their choice and budget before respecting legal rights.

This subject has been the discussion of excellent articles, in an Australian con-text, by John Selby [2000] Ent. LR 1 (page 4), and 2 (page 25).

Defences to Infringement

Aside from the obvious (e.g. there was no substantial copying) there are a number of other defences to copyright infringement. These include the following:

- implied licence (i.e. permission to use the material which can be implied from conduct);

- research and private study;

- criticism, review and news reporting;

- incidental inclusion;

- educational purposes;

- used by libraries and archives

- public policy (see *Hyde Park Residence Ltd* v *Yelland* [1999] RPC 655; *Canon Kabushiki Kaisha* v *Green Cartridge Co (Hong Kong) Ltd* [1997] AC 728.

Further exceptions

There are further exceptions for lawful users (i.e. those with a "right to use" the material: section 50A(2)) as created by an amendment to the Act (by virtue of sections 50A to 50D). These are as follows:

- Section 50A: back up copies. A lawful user may make back up copies of the material of which it is necessary to have.

- Section 50B: decompilation. A lawful user may convert a program to a higher level language and if in doing so he incidentally copies it, that is also permitted. This is only so permitted for this express purpose and only if it is necessary.

- Any contractual term to the contrary of the above exceptions is void by virtue of section 296A.

- Section 50C: other permitted acts. Lawful users are permitted to copy or adapt a program provided that the copying is necessary for his lawful use and is not prohibited under any term of contract.

- Section 50D: acts permitted in relation to databases. A person who has a right to use the database may do anything which is necessary for the purposes of access to and use of the contents of the database. Any contractual term to the contrary being void by virtue of section 296A. Note this is in relation to the copyright of the database and not the database right referred to elsewhere in this chapter.

The Future, Europe and Beyond

Given the diverse laws and yet unifying markets, there has been some international cohesion in forming the World Intellectual Property Organisation Treaty 1996 (WIPO). The Treaty was aimed at providing copyright holders with slightly more control over the material. The Treaty has in some ways been eclipsed by the Copyright Directive which provides a greater degree of information and likely control. The Directive is obviously aimed at the protection of intellectual property and the encouragement of investment into research and development. If the internet strips the ingenious from the profit of their ideas, it will not be long before the creativity and effort behind such ideas dries up. Therefore the pendulum has now, it is suggested, swung back towards protecting property.

There is provision, however, for exemption where temporary acts of reproduction are merely part of a technological process in transmissions or other lawful use which have no independent economic significance.

It is clear that this is a developing area. Watch this space for future developments as the courts will have to determine cases under the wealth of national and increasingly international, law and policy.

TRADE MARKS

A trade mark is a sign, represented graphically, that is capable of distinguishing the goods and services of one undertaking from another (see section 1 Trade Marks Act 1994). The registered mark is defined as a "property right" (see section 2(1)) and therefore may be sold or transferred as other property rights. They also may be protected from infringement in the same manner allowing claims for injunctions or damages.

The law relating to trade marks is aimed, much like passing off (see below), to protect such marks and the obvious intangible value which they possess. Often research and design costs for a particular slogan or piece of packaging will shadow the costs for the actual manufacture of the product itself. The definition of a mark is therefore extremely wide. That does not mean that registration of marks is open to "first come first served" no matter what the mark is. To allow such an approach would soon stifle competition and freedom of expression as even the most generic terms became a corporation's possession. In order to register the mark certain hurdles must be overcome (see below).

The width of the definition obviously brings with it the complexity surrounding computer information. It has been recognised that the definition "would appear also to extend to such ephemera as sounds and smells and, perhaps, even graphical computer user interfaces" (see 2.600, *Encyclopedia of Information Technology*, Sweet & Maxwell).

In order to define what is capable of being registered as a mark one has to apply a process of elimination. By identifying what is incapable of being registered, the opposite is obtainable. Having firmly in mind the principles of registration will allow a much greater appreciation of the width of this subject.

Principles of Registration

The first and most important thing to note about the registration of trade marks is that it is a statutory creature not dependant upon the creation of any mark, nor originality. We have seen above that copyright is usually associated purely with the creation of some novel and new material. Instead, trade mark law will protect the person / corporate whom first registers the mark (subject to meeting the criteria for registration).

Refusal of registration may either be absolute and therefore mandatory (section 3) or relative (section 5). The absolute grounds of registration are as follows:

(a) those that are not a "sign capable of being represented graphically which is capable of distinguishing goods or services of one undertaking from those of other undertakings";

(b) those that are "devoid of any distinctive character";

(c) those that "consist exclusively of signs or indications which may serve, in trade, to designate the kind, quality, quantity, intended purpose, value, geographical origin, the time of production of goods or of rendering of services, or other characteristics of goods or services";

(d) those which "consist exclusively of signs or indications which have become customary in the current language or in the *bona fide* and established practices of the trade";

(e) those which result exclusively from the shape which is
(i) resulting from the nature of the goods themselves,
(ii) necessary to obtain a technical result, or
(iii) the reason why the goods have substantial value;

(f) those which are contrary to public policy, morality or are likely to deceive the public;

(g) it is a specially protected emblem or contrary to any enactment or the application is made in bad faith.

Provided that before the application to register the applicant has, in fact, acquired a distinctive character by the use of the mark, (b), (c) and (d) will not operate as a bar to registration (see section 3(1)).

The relative grounds for refusal are identified in section 5 and outlined as follows. Registration will be refused if the owner of the earlier mark / right does not consent, and:

(a) the mark is identical to one already registered for the identical class of product / service;

(b) the mark is identical / similar to one already registered for a similar class of product / service for the identical / similar product if there exists a likelihood of confusion on the part of the public (including the likelihood of association with the earlier mark);

(c) the mark is identical / similar to an earlier trade mark and it is to be registered for dissimilar goods / services but the use of the later mark without due cause would take unfair advantage of, or be detrimental to, the distinctive character or the repute of the earlier trade mark;

(d) the use of the mark is liable to be prevented by any rule of law (e.g. passing off, copyright).

To summarise, the law of trade marks is there to protect the use of slogans, packaging, symbols, colours, sounds, etc, which have been formulated to create an image which is not related purely to the product / service itself and will not stifle free competition and expression. Names such as "baked beans" are plainly not capable of registration as it is merely descriptive of what the product is. If it were capable of registration this would act as a fetter for other manufacturers to describe to the consumer what it is that they are purchasing.

Registration is made against certain classes of marks (for example "computer program"). There is no distinction between goods and services. Those wishing to protect their right to certain marks are advised to clearly label any marks (registered or not) as being possessed by the proprietor. This will prevent the mark becoming generic or its use becoming saturated and the mark losing its distinctiveness.

One factor which is strikingly important for those using the internet / e-mail network is to achieve protection wherever the mark is published. So, for instance, applications may be necessary in all countries whereby users have access to the mark. Certain practical arrangements have made some applications unnecessary. These are complex matters and the user of a mark is well advised to check the current situation before embarking upon registration. However, the most relevant agreements / conventions in force at present are as follows:

(a) *The Community Trade Mark Regulation:* single registration creates a right which covers the European Union.

(b) *The Madrid Agreement / Protocol:* allowing an international registration of marks.

(c) *The Paris Convention:* Allows registration of a priority date to be back-dated so long as certain requirements are met. Also provides for the use of a trade name to be treated as a trade mark.

Infringement of a Trade Mark used in the Course of Trade

A trade mark will be infringed if the use of an identical mark is used in relation to identical goods or services (section 10(1)).

There will also be an infringement whereby the use of an identical or similar mark is used for identical or similar goods and services would lead to the likelihood of confusion on the part of the public (see section 10(2)). Further, under section 10(3) there will be an infringement if a sign which is identical or similar to the mark and is used in relation to dissimilar goods but the mark has a reputation in the UK and the use of the sign without due cause would take unfair advantage of, or be detrimental to, the distinctive character or the repute of the trade mark.

In a recent case Neuberger J. considered sections 10(2) and (3) (*Premier Brands UK Ltd* v *Typhoon Europe and anor* [2000] All ER (D) 52). There the owner of the mark was TYPHOO which had the mark registered under various different classes. The use of the sign "TYPHOON" for kitchenware was in issue. The colouring of the two were similar, aside from the rather obvious similarity of the letters. Under section 10(2) it was held that the lack of any likelihood of confusion was fatal to the claim of infringement. Under section 10(3) it was held that there was no destructive element present by virtue of the association with powerful storms and that the products would not be blurred such as to cause any unfair advantage or otherwise. The case therefore foundered on the fact that in reality there was unlikely to be any confusion, association or unfair advantage.

Defences

The main available defences which are open are as follows:

(1) Honest comparative advertising (e.g. NONAME Internet Service Provider charges you £X for its service which comprises A, B, and C. We at NOBODY Internet Service Provider charge you £X for our new expanded service, incorporating A, B, C, D and E).

(2) Legitimate use prior to the Trade Marks Act 1994 came into effect;

(3) Where the owner is said to have "acquiesced" (i.e. for a period of five continuous years with knowledge of the use): section 48;

(4) Honest use of a person's own name or address;

(5) Exploitation of an earlier right (e.g. passing off);

(6) Honest use of a mark to indicate purpose for which it is intended for;

(7) Honest use of descriptive indications.

It is also possible to seek a declaration / injunction from the Court that threats regarding marks are groundless and should be restrained: see section 21.

Issues Relating to E-mail and Internet

Domain Names

Domain names indicate part of the name or address of a site on the internet. Often these will be registered trade marks in themselves. The use of the domain name may be restricted and there is some value in being the first to register the domain name (see for example *Prince plc* v *Prince Sports Group Inc.* [1998] FSR 21.

In *Avnet Inc.* v *Isoact Limited* [1998] FSR 16 the defendant used the domain name "Avnet" which was incidentally registered as a trade mark by the claimant. The claim was not upheld on the basis that the services which were being provided were different in the defendant's case than they were in the claimant's case. As a result of which Jacob J. held that there was no infringement. It shows that the courts will be keen to avoid a wide and protective approach to registered marks and that there is no guaranteed right to a domain name where the trademark in the same name is registered.

It is also noted that the confusion which may have resulted from any initial search engine is not sufficient to attract trademark law (the surfer would then instantly realise his/her mistake: see the discussion on this subject at page 141, *Law & the Internet* (Edited by Lillian Edwards and Charlotte Waelde, 2000, 2nd edition). This is of relevance to section 10(2). However, see below for more discussion on the relevance of search engines.

A broad approach was taken to protecting trademarks from confusion in *Canon Kabushiki Kaisha* v *MGM* Case C-39/37, [1998] All ER (EC) 934. Therein the court held that the similarity of goods heavily depended on the distinctiveness and reputation of the marks.

Of relevance to section 10(3) (i.e. the prevention of dilution), but more importantly passing off (see below), it has been held that distinctive marks contained within domain names should be handed back to the holders of such distinctive marks (see *BT and others* v *One in a Million and others* [1999] 4 All ER 476. The decision is wide in its ambit).

In *MBNA Amercian Bank NA* v *Freeman* (Ch. Div. unrep. 17 July 2000) Nicholas Strauss QC was faced with an application for an interlocutory injunction by virtue of an alleged improper use of a trade mark pursuant to section 10(3)(b) of the Act. In granting the interim remedy it was of importance that the sale of the domain name was possibly an improper use of goodwill. The sale of the site could lead to an irrecoverable claim for damages or for an account of profit. The interlocutory injunction was granted and the defendant would have to apply to the court before selling or dealing with the name prior to trial. The case demonstrates the possible use of interlocutory remedies in this area of law and the effectiveness of those remedies prior to trial. Any such remedy should be sought as a matter of urgency.

Users are not just subject to court action. In *Winterson* v *Hogarth* [2000] ETMR 783 the WIPO Administrative Panel found that the registering of an author's name was made in bad faith and transferred the domain name to the author concerned. The Uniform Domain Name Dispute Resolution Policy, paragraph 4, required the author to show that the user had registered an identical or confusingly similar domain name to the trade or service mark. Importantly, the mark did not have to be registered and could include the author's name alone. In *Christian Dior Coutre SA* v *Liage International Inc.* [2000] ETMR 773, the notoriety of the mark in question qualified for extended protection under Article 16(3) of the Agreement on Trade Related Aspects of Intellectual Property Rights including Trade in Counterfeit Goods (TRIPs) (see also Paris Convention Art.6 bis).

The law has not sufficiently settled in this area to make any detailed commentary useful. It has however, reflected the general common sense view that property rights should be protected where there is no good reason not to do so. For instance, it is submitted that the fair result was achieved in both of the above cases despite the opportunity to criticise the reasoning leading to the final result.

Meta – Tags

Meta-tags are the list of words that describe a web-site. This book may, for example, be listed as "book / internet / e-mail / law / trade marks" etc. The search engines will then pick up in the entered words and display the end result. There has been some litigation abut the use of trade marks in Meta – Tags. Essentially the present result seem to be that trade marks cannot be used where there will be some confusion. This is evidenced by the US Playboy cases (see *Playboy Enterprises Inc.* v *Universal Tel-A-Talk Inc* ED Pa No 96–6961 11/4/98; *Playboy Enterprises Inc.* v *AsiaFocus Inc.* ED Va Civil Action No. 97–734-A 4/28/98 and *Playboy Enterprises Inc.* v *Welles* SD Cal Case No 98-CV-0413-K (JFS) 4/22/98).

The recent case of *Roadtech Computer Systems Ltd* v *Mandata (Management and Data Services) Ltd* [2000] LTL 22 June highlighted the issue in the context of a passing-off action (for which see below). It involved the use of meta-tags. The claimant claimed in a passing-off action that the defendant was diverting business from its own web-site by using what the claimant claimed to be its meta-tags. Master Bowman held, among other things, that the use of the claimant's website was a deliberate, albeit unsophisticated, appropriation of R's rights and damages were awarded accordingly. It is important to note that the meta-tags used by Mandata were registered trade marks of Roadtech (see above, under Trade Marks for more discussion on this subject).

This effectively recognised meta-tags as part of a companies' intellectual property.

Only time will tell what other intangible property rights will be recognised in the future as technology and the law develops.

EXAMPLE

Scrumpy king Bruce Baker owns the multi-national cider-making company 'Scrumptious Bumptious' which name he has registered as a trade mark. Based in Alcombe, he sells his world-renowned cider through his web-site: *www.oooaaarrr.com*. The metatags which he has listed include: cider, scrumpy, scrumptious, bumptious, oooaaarrr. His main competitor, international playboy Clive Bryan, owns 'Bryan's Brews'. He has fallen behind Bruce Baker due to the success of the latter's web-site. In order to try and counter this success, Clive Bryan sets up his own web-site *www.baintbebad.com*. In his list of metatags he includes the words 'scrumptious' and 'bumptious' in order to try and divert customers to his own web-site.

Has Clive Bryan appropriated Bruce Baker's rights in the name Scrumptious Bumptious?

E-mail Message allegedly emanating from another

Trade marks can be infringed where e-mails are sent with a trade mark giving rise to confusion as to their source. Such infringement will probably be actionable: see *Hotmail* v *Van$ Money Pie Inc*. 47 USPQ 2d 1020 (ND Cal 1998).

It remains to be seen the true extent of trade mark law in cyberspace. Notably, it is suggested that the principles of trade mark law are kept firmly in mind when dealing with this novel area. The UK's jurisprudence is limited hitherto, but some indication of what the future holds can be seen from the USA, that future being more litigation!

PASSING OFF

This area of law is the common law sister of trade marks. In essence the law aims to protect the reputation of goods, services or trade names of any person / corporation built upon their goodwill. Therefore an action will lie if someone attempts to "pass off" their own goods as if the same or connected to the original creator / owner.

Given that the rights exist in the common law, there is no requirement (as opposed to Trade Mark law) to register any mark.

There are basically five elements of passing off which must be shown to establish the tort. These are as follows:

(1) that there was a misrepresentation (not necessarily fraudulent or negligent);

(2) that it was made in the course of trade;

(3) to prospective customers of his or ultimate consumers of goods, etc, supplied by him;

(4) that it is reasonably foreseeable that a consequence will be injury to business or goodwill of another trader;

(5) which causes, or is likely to cause, actual damage to the business or goodwill of the trader in the UK market.

(see the important House of Lords' decision of *Warninck* v *Townend* [1980] R.P.C. 31 at 105–6, known commonly as the "Advocaat" case).

Perhaps the most important aspect behind the tort is that of confusion. There must be some element of the possibility of customers confusing the two suppliers. If there is no confusion, then the goods, etc, are not being "passed off" as another's. For examples of the same see *Harrods Ltd* v *Harrodian School* [1996] R.P.C. 697 and *Lego Systems A/S* v *Lego M Lemelstrich Ltd* [1983] F.S.R. 155.

A case closer to the issues within this book is *Hammond Suddards* v *Limetime Limited* [1991] 4 E.I.P.R. 73 whereby the claimant's offered on-line debt collection services trading as "Debtline". A software house was successfully sued when producing a computer program under the same name. The court held that there was a real risk of confusion.

Further, in *Logica plc* v *Logo Logica (UK) Ltd* (Ch. Div. Unrep. 7 August 2000) Neuberger J. granted summary judgment and injunctive relief. The claimant was a company offering IT services from its web-site. These services included the design of web-sites. The defendant was a new business proposing to enter into graphic design services and argued that they were not connected with computers. Neuberger J. held that the marks were almost identical and that in today's current technological climate it would be highly unlikely that the defendant's business would be conducted without catering to internet and computer users. There was obviously serious scope for confusion.

Goodwill can be limited to a national area or international. Users on the internet can be confused by the origin of products more easily over the internet than in conventional settings. In *New Zealand Post Ltd* v *Leng* [1998–99] Info. T.L.R. 233 it was held that confusion could exist where the customer is using search engines to find a certain product/service.

Companies operating over the internet must be very careful in the way that goods and services are marketed. It is increasingly easier to market goods to a wide customer base without really *entering* the market. This does not mean that the law has been relaxed in any way for e-businesses and it is essential, therefore, that e-businesses evaluate the market that they seek to enter before launching products whereby there may be some confusion. Confusion is a nebulous concept and therefore will depend on the facts of each case. For instance, a global business will be far more likely to enter into new markets than small localised businesses. Therefore, the use, in a new market, of a well known multi-faceted company name, will be more likely to amount to an infringement than that of a localised single product company.

In the context of the fast moving and easily obtainable internet information highway, it is essential that all parties seeking to protect their marks, etc, must keep a clear record of the history of their mark and when they first published the same. Customer logs and all companies using the prospective claimant's goods, services or marks must be kept in order to show the timing and access to the claimant's goods and services. Otherwise the rights against passing off may only be of theory value as the evidence to pursue the claim will be sadly lacking.

Similar issues will arise under passing off as with Trade Marks and the reader is reminded of the above discussion.

PATENTS

The law relating to patents is more traditionally concerned with inventions and the protection of, for instance, machinery. The protection that a patent gives is not indefinite and is limited to a period of years to allow the patentee to profit from the work that has been expended but not so long as to stifle the market and place an unnecessary burden upon science.

The granting of patents and their enforcement is subject to careful regulation. This is for good reason, as a patent is effectively a legally enforceable monopoly. However, it does have a positive side for the public at large. It encourages the disclosure of how the invention works and therefore allows, in the long term, development of science. There is in effect a trade – if you tell me how you made it, I will allow you to exploit it under a monopoly.

Patents covering the UK can be obtained through the British Office or the European Patent Office (for all of Europe). A patent granted by the EPO designating the UK will be read as if granted under the Patents Act 1977 (section 77).

On the date that an application is made the patent will be judged against the state of the art to see whether in fact it is capable of receiving a patent. The date when it is so judged is known as the "priority date". The "priority date" may be sooner where there is an earlier application claimed. The patent will last for 20 years.

Patentable Items

Items which are patentable are not explicitly defined by statute. However, this area of law is certainly aimed at inventions rather than ideas or information (covered more appropriately by other forms of intellectual property). Professor Cornish suggests that

> "Two main ideas recur in distinguishing the categories of subject-matter that may and may not be patented. One is that intellectual conceptions become patentable only to the extent that they have been embodied in technical applications. The other is that techniques which relate to living organisms, animal or vegetable, may call for special treatment: either because the public interest demands that their use should not be restricted or because a special legislative regime is needed for their protection."
>
> (W.R. Cornish, *Intellectual Property: Patents, Copyright, Trade Marks and Allied Rights*, Fourth edition at 5–55).

The concept is difficult to describe explicitly and it may well be a case of being able to recognise one when you see it, but not being able to coherently describe it beforehand. There has been great difficulty in the area of computer programs. Mathematical calculations and formulas have not, in the past, been considered as capable of registration. However, this is in effect what computer programs are. This has lead to some confusion as to the nature of the current law. This is a matter which will no doubt receive judicial attention in the near future, as more and more technological advancement is taking place. The most recent pronouncement of note has been from the EPO Technical Board of Appeal in cases T0935/97, T1173/97:

> "In the view of the Board, a computer program claimed by itself is not excluded from patentability if the program, when running on a computer or loaded into a computer, brings about, or is capable of bringing about, a technical effect which goes beyond the "normal" physical interactions between the program (software) and the computer (hardware) on which it is run."

It was furthermore accepted that the technical character of an invention was generally required before it was patentable. Of considerable importance to this work was that the Board suggested that it made no difference whether a computer programme is claimed by itself or as a record on a carrier, and that further there may be no need to have reference to a carrier. Thus, as noted by the editors of the *Encyclopaedia of Information Technology Law*, this "would appear to give considerable flexibility in determining claims appropriate to provide coverage for an invention, for example for a software-implemented invention distributed on line over the Internet" (at Release 25).

As a result of the aforementioned case, the UK patent office and the EPO have issued guidance notes. Such guidance accepts the reasoning in the above case and state that patents will be granted where it is shown that the program produces a technical effect which is more than would follow merely on the running of a program on a computer and which is such that claims to the computer when programmed would not be rejected under the current law (summary of the UK guidance). The EPO guidance refers to the technical effect as going beyond the normal physical interaction between program and computer.

Property Right

Patents are a property right and can be transferred or assigned. They vest in the inventor who is usually easy enough to establish. Inventions created whilst in the course of employment remain the invention of the employer: section 39. Those created whilst on a contract for services (e.g. computer consultant) will not belong to the employer unless expressly provided for in the contract.

Requirements for a Patent

The Patents Act 1977 ("the Act") provides that in order to be capable of receiving a patent, an invention must be:

(1) novel;

(2) involving an inventive step;

(3) is capable of industrial application.

Further, the registration must not be restricted on other grounds (see below).

Novelty demands that the invention is not already known in the public domain. It must be outside the current state of the art and must not have been anticipated (by, for instance, drawings and photographs in the public domain). Thus the proliferation of information over the internet must be treated with care if inventors wish to have their work patented, then it is prudent to not release any details of the invention until their rights under the Act is assured. The internet's vast audience may well lead to inventions becoming public knowledge at the touch of a button.

If there is enough material for an invention to be figured out in the public domain, then this will be a bar to registration. The test for showing novelty is perhaps higher than at first sight appears the case. The public domain is taken to include specialists in the field (see *Stahlwerk Becker's Patent* (1919) 36 RPC 13, where the House of Lords decided that the marketing of steel amounted to publication of the composition of the same as it could be deduced by chemical analysis).

Mixtures and selections (e.g. for chemical substances) have sometimes been allowed, though it is true to say that they are probably rare (see 5–23, W R

Cornish, *Intellectual Property: Patents, Copyright, Trade Marks and Allied Rights,* fourth edition).

"Inventive step" is satisfied where it can be demonstrated that having regard to the state of the art, the invention is not obvious to someone skilled in the art concerned (see section 3 and Article 56 of the European Patent Convention). Effectively the law will recognise when an inventor has taken something a step forward, but will not recognise minor alterations or improvements. It is essentially a question of fact and degree.

In relation to the requirement to have industrial application this can be made out where it can be made or used in any type of industry including agriculture (section 4(1)). Importantly an invention of a method of treatment of the human or animal body by surgery or therapy or of a diagnosis practised on the human or animal body shall not be taken to be capable of industrial application (section 4(2)). This section protects from monopoly the advancement of medicine and treatment.

Infringement

The grant of a patent is the grant of an exclusive right of monopoly over the subject matter. Thus any use of the patent subject matter by another in the course of trade may be prevented (see section 60). In the course of trade can include preparatory stages in the use of a patentable subject matter / process for an eventual commercial gain. Infringement can also be indirect, that is when the party concerned supplies in the UK "with any of the means, relating to an essential element of the invention, for putting the invention into effect when he knows, or it is obvious to a reasonable person in the circumstances, that those means are suitable for putting, and are intended to put, the inventions into effect in the United Kingdom" (section 60(2)). This concept is known as indirect infringement and has been noted as important in the field of computer related inventions whereby the information on disk may not be covered as such, but is an essential element of the invention (see chapter 4 *Computer Law*, 4th ed. Edited by Chris Reed and John Angel). Of note is the fact that both the place of supply and the place where it is intended to carry out the invention must be the UK.

A full range of remedies is available including injunctions, delivery up, damages and account of profits.

DESIGN RIGHTS

This subject is partially covered by the law of copyright (above). However, there exists certain free standing rights by virtue of the Registered Designs Act

1949 (25 years protection for non-functional designs) and the design right as protected by section 213(1) of the Copyright, Designs and Patents Act 1988. The design right is protected as a property right.

Scope of Protection

Section 213(1) provides that there shall be protection for original designs. Design is defined as "the design of any aspect of the shape or configuration (whether internal or external) of the whole or part of any article". Under section 213(4) it makes it clear that the design must not be common in the field of such designs.

Much like with trade marks, design rights which are capable of receiving protection are ascertainable more by those which do not amount to such a status rather than by any explicit inclusive list. By section 213(3) the following are not capable of attracting protection:

(a) a method/principle of construction;

(b) those designs which copy aspects of another product / item which it is meant to attach to or form an integral part of. For instance a power lead will need to copy its source if it is to fit into it;

(c) designs amounting only to surface decoration.

The right exists when it is recorded in a design document (similar to copyright). The designer will normally own the design subject to the rules relating to employment (see the Patents section above) and any written agreement to the contrary.

The creation of a design by a computer will be traced back to the person who set up the computer with the arrangements necessary for the creation of the final product.

Infringement

The owner of the design right enjoys a commercial monopoly on the same both in the design document itself and in the making of the articles from the design. Remedies are as outlined with patents, above.

The duration of a design right is the shorter of:

(a) 15 years from the end of the year of creation; or

(b) 10 years from the end of the year in which articles made from the design are available for sale.

THE FUTURE

EU Design Right Directive

The liability of ISPs and telecommunications companies has been considered throughout this work in varying different places. The E.U. has been developing the law on the liability of intermediaries, and most importantly for this work, the liability of ISPs. The E.U. Design Rights Directive has been drafted and approved which must be implemented by Member States by 28 October 2001. This Directive applies to all civil liability but has especial importance to intellectual property. The following are the main effects of the same.

The Directive limits / excludes liability for three types of intermediaries:

(a) a mere conduit will only be required to remove something which is infringing following a court order and no damages will be payable. The words "mere conduit" mean the provider of a communications network who does not

    (i)   initiate the transmission;

    (ii) select the recipient of the transmission; and

    (iii) does not select, or modify, the transmission.

(b) A service provider who caches content will only be required to remove the infringing article by court order and will not be liable in damages unless it has not acted expeditiously in the removal of the infringing article along with knowledge of the infringement. (see also *Godfrey* v *Demon Internet Limited* [1999] 4 All E.R. 342). Such a service provider is someone who caches information if they are involved in the automatic, intermediate and temporary storage of that information performed for the sole purpose of passing that information on more efficiently to those who request it.

(c) A service provider who "hosts" certain information will only be liable if it becomes aware of the infringing material and fails to act expeditiously to remove it.

It should be noted that an E.U. wide design right regulation is still in draft. Watch this space!

Peer-to-peer systems

This is said to be one of the pointers to future communications on the net. The most famous example of a peer-to-peer ('P2P') system is Napster which basically gave its members access to all of its other members' music stored on their computers when they were on-line. An American court has found Napster to be illegal but the site was kept open pending appeal and in the meantime Bertelsmann, a German media group announced an alliance with the purpose of turning Napster into a "secure membership-based service" that pays fees to artists and record labels.

P2P is in reality nothing more than the internet returning to its roots as a "networks of equals connected directly, without going through a hub" (*The Economist*, 4 November 2000, page 109). However, with the rise of 'always-on' internet connection computers (through, for example, ADSL), P2P may well be on the rise. Aimster allows AOL instant message users to limit the size of their file-sharing group. Gnutella and Gonesilent.com are variations on the Napster theme. Gonesilent.com is developing software that enables users to search for files directly on other PCs.

Clearly, these developments will create significant challenges for the law of intellectual property both domestically and perhaps more importantly supranationally. A particular difficulty will be that the use of new internal computer systems may mean that it is difficult, if not impossible, to track the source of intellectual property right infringements.

CHAPTER 9
UNSOLICITED MAIL

"Well, there's egg and bacon; egg sausage and bacon; egg and spam; egg bacon and spam; egg bacon sausage and spam; spam bacon sausage and spam; spam egg spam spam bacon and spam; spam sausage spam spam bacon spam tomato and spam".

Terry Jones, Monty Python

INTRODUCTION

Spam may have been an obligatory part of the menu for Eric Idle and Graham Chapman and so it seems it is for all those using e-mail, hence the nick-name.

This chapter sets out a brief guide to the law and practice in this area and draws in particular upon the US experience.

GENERAL

Such unsolicited bulk e-mails are increasingly becoming a problem given the ease with which such correspondence may be made. Precedents had already been set with the use of bulk faxes but the effect has been felt much more widely with e-mail due to the fact that many more people have a personal e-mail address than fax number coupled with the low cost of sending an e-mail.

Consumers dislike spam because it effectively shifts the cost of advertising onto them as they effectively have to pay to download the message. ISPs dislike it because it clogs up their systems and slows the traffic down by reducing storage space and bandwidth. In a US case, e-mail that would normally have been delivered in minutes, took three days (*CompuServe Incorporated* v *Cyber Promotions, Inc. and Sandford Wallace, No. C2–96–1070* (S.D. Ohio Oct. 24 1996)). Because the sender of the e-mail is often disguised (cloaking), the systems are unable to identify where to return undeliverable messages, further cutting their capacity. Reduced performance creates irate customers who may move to another provider in what is a highly competitive market. (See article by Jeremy Drew at [1998] 9 SCL 4).

THE US EXPERIENCE

Judicial

The article reports that in the US there have been numerous successful court proceedings by service providers against spammers, from which common principles can be identified (such as *CompuServe Inc.* v *Cyber Promotions, Inc.* No 962F. Supp.1015 (S.D. Ohio Feb.3, 1997)). In March 1998 a $2,000,000 consent judgment against a spammer was reported (*Earthlink Networks* v *Cyber Promotions, Inc.* No BC 167502 (Cal. Super. Ct. L.A. County, Mar. 30. 1998)).

The courts have decided that spam e-mail can constitute a trespass of the service provider's personal property, because of the degradation in the system's performance. This can justify an injunction against the spammer, provided he has received notice that he is trespassing.

Other effective arguments have been based on registered trademark infringement/passing-off where, for example, the e-mail has been 'spoofed' by using a registered/unregistered trademark.

Recently, *www.theregister.co.uk* (Lucy Sherriff, 12 December 2000) reported that a man who spammed millions of AOL subscribers with pornography and get-rich-quick schemes has pleaded guilty to second-degree forgery in a US District court. The man, of Mission Viejo, California, admitted that he took over a Westchester company's Internet service to send the unsolicited mails, which he disguised to make appear as though they had come from IBM's Internet provider, IBM.net.

On 3 January 2001, John Leyden in the same publication reported that two Los Angeles men are to go to jail for their part in a bulk e-mail scam which duped 12,000 people and severely impacted the operations of several large US ISPs. The spam messages sent out by the gang invited recipients to send a £24 "processing fee" in order to learn how to get a job stuffing envelopes. 12,000 people replied to the scam which was perhaps particularly surprising given that such jobs are advertised in almost every evening newspaper's situation vacant column.

The law has also been utilised by those who are wrongly accused of spamming. On 17 November 2000, Lucy Sherriff of *www.theregister.co.uk* reported that a US District Court in Denver had issued a temporary restraining order on behalf of on-line marketing gurus, 24/7, against the Mail Abuse Prevention System (MAPS). 24/7 Media went to the court after MAPS included its subsidiary, 24/7 Exactis, in the spammers blacklist the Real Time Blackhole List. The list, it was reported, is used by many ISPs to determine whether or not to block mail coming from a particular address. The District Judge John Kane found that MAPS had been irresponsible in adding 24/7 Exactis to the RBL. He ordered MAPS and any others acting in concert with MAPS to remove 24/7 Media from the RBL, and to rescind any comments to ISPs that state or suggest that 24/7 Media sends spam. He also found that the inclusion of 24/7 on the RBL actually meant some people did not get e-mails they had requested.

Legislative

Finally, there has been legislative provision in the US. On 11 June 1998, a law was passed in Washington to regulate, to a certain extent, the sending of unsolicited commercial e-mail providing for damages to be payable (*Engrossed Substitute House Bill 2752 – 25 March 1998*). There are similar bills waiting at national level, and a continued drive to get laws passed at Federal level. These will help avoid the need to fit e-mail activity within the constraints of the existing laws of trespass.

Private sector

MAPS, referred to above, is itself a good example of how the private sector have started to deal with spam. It is a California non-profit organisation which maintains a database of spammers.

However, this in itself has resulted in a steady accumulation of lawsuits by those who believe MAPS is interfering with their businesses.

In addition, at present systems such as MAPS may potentially cause difficulties with legitimate mail on a particular server. On 16 November 2000, Thomas C. Greene reported in *www.theregister.co.uk* that MAPS had published a bulletin reporting that Microsoft's ISP and portals, MSN had become easy prey for spammers due to several poorly-protected mail (SMTP) servers to which outsiders can connect easily for a free, anonymous ride. MAPS placed the several mail servers in question on its Relay Spam Stopper (RSS) list, until MSN can manage to correct the problem.

In this case, MAPS caused some difficulty with legitimate mail on the MSN network, which it said it could do nothing about because the RSS could not be tweaked with enough precision to avoid throwing out the baby with the bath water. The compromise here is to block all traffic from individual servers clearly associated with large quantities of spam. Unfortunately, this is the only way to defeat the offending pink substance with any degree of confidence, as rules-based filters are even less precise, often stopping a good deal more legitimate mail.

MAPS were reported to have already received several complaints from those whose regular mail has been interrupted as a result of adding MSN to the

RSS. They recommended applying pressure on MSN to get its act together quickly.

THE UK

Judicial

In this area it is unclear how the UK courts will deal with the issue. Certainly the laws of trespass, as found in the Torts (Interference with Goods) Act 1977, are similar to those in the US.

Existing laws on infringement of registered trademarks and passing-off would be readily applicable and there may also be arguments available under the Computer Misuse Act 1990 in respect of unauthorised modification of computer material and under the Data Protection Act 1998 with regard to use of the e-mail address. Potentially the Protection from Harassment Act 1997 may also come into play in the future with regard to cyber-stalkers.

Most of these issues are dealt with in other chapters of this book.

In addition to consumers' remedies, service providers should ensure that they have provided against spamming in their terms and conditions and that they are technologically equipped to deal swiftly and efficiently with spammers.

Legislative

As regards legislative progress, the Telecommunications (Data Protection and Privacy) (Direct Marketing) Regulations 1998, SI 1998/3170 implemented the Telecommunications Privacy Directive 97/66/EC (OJ 1998 L 24/1). They include the prohibition on using automated calling machines or faxes as a means of direct marketing without the consent of the subscriber (Regulations 6 and 8). However, they do not provide for unsolicited e-mails. See also The Telecommunications (Data Protection and Privacy) Regulations 1999.

The Distance Selling Directive dealt with in Chapter 19 below follow a similar pattern in only permitting the use of automated calling machines and faxes with prior consent.

Finally, the Electronic Commerce Directive 2000/31/EC, L178; [2000] OJ 17 July (*http://europa.eu.int/comm/internal_market/en/media/eleccomm/com31en.pdf*) provides that service providers undertaking unsolicited commercial communications by e-mail should regularly consult and respect opt-out registers in which natural persons not wishing to receive such commercial communications have registered (article 7(2)). Further, any unsolicited Commercial Communication must be clearly and unequivocally identifiable as such as soon as it is received by the recipient (Article 7(1)). This might require a statement of its nature appearing in the header that appears on the screen. This Directive is dealt with in more detail in Chapter 20, below.

The recent debate with regard to legislation for unsolicited e-mails in this country at present is whether the system should be an 'opt-out' or an 'opt-in' one. A discussion of this debate may be found in an article by Professor Geraint G. Howells at NLJ 972 2000.

It remains to be seen how the government will respond to the problem.

The need for action will perhaps become even more acute as spamming becomes more common with mobile phones. On 14 November 2000, Kieren McCarthy in *www.theregister.co.uk* reported that Vodafone and the Data Protection Commissioner had joined forces in an attempt to shut down a mobile spam company, Webcom International. The two of them claimed that the company was abusing the SMS service and breaking data protection rules. Not so, said Webcom, which reportedly sends out four million spam text messages a week, they dial numbers randomly and so no rules have been broken. Vodafone was unswayed and wanted the company shut down. Following one conversation with the Data Commissioner, Webcom agreed to make it clear that the message was an advertisement. Interestingly, it claims that 30 per cent of people that receive the junk message respond to it.

For further analysis of cross-border transactions, see Part 4 of this book.

CHAPTER 10
VIRUSES, HACKING AND SAFER SURFING

INTRODUCTION

Unsolicited mail is commonly the agent for the transmission of computer viruses and the tool of computer hackers. According to a recent survey by Datamonitor (*www.datamonitor.com*), the business information group, financial loss caused by security breaches to e-businesses costs more than $15 billion (£11 billion) each year. As the *Daily Telegraph* reported on 16 November 2000:

> "The report found that more than 50pc of businesses worldwide spent just 5pc or less of their information technology (IT) budget on securing their networks. Recent security breaches such as the I LOVE YOU virus has clearly not scared companies into taking sufficient preventative action."

This chapter provides a brief guide to the law and practice in this area and in particular to some of the technical aspects of viruses.

THE LOVE BUG AND THE GOOD TIMES WARNING

Perhaps the one positive aspect of the now infamous 'Love' bug is that it alerted the wider public to the dangers of computer viruses. However, the virus was in fact very basic. Once the e-mail was opened, all that it in fact did was to send out the same e-mail to all of the recipient's address book. It does not appear that it was any more intrusive than that.

Furthermore, it does not seem that people have learnt that much in terms of their practice given how common the prevalence of the Good Times type e-mail even in the last few months. These type of e-mails have been around for years and are characterised by such phrases as "pass this on to all your friends", "passing this on to ten people will bring you luck", "warning: virus alert" or "check that this is true on the x web-site" (and x will be a very large and ever-changing news-site such as cnn.com on which it would be impossible to disprove that the news had been there at some point).

Such e-mails often last for years as they loiter like litter in the virtual world passing slowly from one computer to another. Not all contain viruses and the greatest complaint that may be levelled at many is that they lead to time wasting (hence their nick-name 'thought-contagion' viruses, a term probably deriving from a book by Aaron Lynch entitled 'Thought Contagion'; another more recent name given to them is 'memetic viruses'). Others however, do contain viruses which in some way or other affects the computer system.

Other agents for passing on a new virus include humorous cartoons, photographs or jokes about a particular contemporary world event. Only in hindsight do we perhaps all question whether the e-mail declaring British sovereignty over the United States during the election debacle in 2000 contained any latent viruses.

A report of a hoax e-mail was made in *www.theregister.co.uk* on 2 July 2000 by John Lettice:

> "A bogus email sent out to Hotmail users claims they'll be cut off if they don't prove they're using their accounts. In order to do so, all they've got to do is forward the email to other Hotmail users … The message purports to be from one Jon Henard of Hotmail, and claims the service has too many customers. This does have some plausibility, as Hotmail has 68 million, and some free services do actually kick you off if you go quiet for too long. Hotmail itself does this after 90 days, but more widespread sackings would surely be a cull too far. The mechanism too is tried and tested. Chain emails have a long, inglorious and largely harmless history on the net, one of the best and most durable being the old Walt Disney Jr and Microsoft scam, which purports to offer users rewards for co-operating in the development of an email tracking system. We mention this one largely as an attempt to reduce the number of tip-offs we get about it every year, but it has a certain elegance – it's the sort of 1984 plot you just *want* to believe is real. The latest Hotmail one differs of course in that it uses fear, rather than the usual greed, as impetus …®"

HTML BUG

This was described in an article by Thomas C. Greene in *www.theregister.co.uk* on 11 December 2000:

> "We recently came across an InfoWorld.com item suggesting that an HTML 'bug' implanted in spam could be a major boon to malicious hackers. The technique mentioned involves embedding a link to a

tiny, one-pixel image on the spammer's server. When victim retrieves the message, his e-mail client automatically fetches the image off the spammer's server in order to display it in the message window. Since the image is miniscule, the victim never sees it and never suspects that his client is communicating with a remote server. The logs then tell the spammer which e-mail addys or IPs connected to his server looking for the image, which in turn tells him which e-mail addresses are valid, and thus he keeps them on his victim list. All this is pretty smarmy; it means that spammers can verify valid e-mail addresses with decent accuracy. The normal defensive techniques of not following any link in a spam message and never replying to the decoy "remove me" address (which, far from getting you removed, only confirms that your address works), would no longer be effective. It's also possible, with JavaScript or ActiveX, to use this basic technique to launch an involuntary browser session pointing to a malicious site, during which a cookie can be dropped on the victim's drive and with which his moves can be tracked. It would also not be tricky to use the HTML bug to generate a cookie where e-mail HTML is rendered by the browser. But we're not convinced that the specific technique cited – merely embedding a one-pixel image on the body of a spam message – could give malicious hackers remote access to a network or machine, or anything else that they couldn't get more easily through other means. However, the possibility is suggested in the *InfoWorld* piece: "It's just a matter of time [before] someone [can] figure out how to use these things against people or corporations," the paper quotes Sharon Ward, director of enterprise business applications at Hurwitz Group, as saying." ..."

TROJAN HORSES

It does not take much to imagine a bug with the distribution of the love bug but with Trojan horse capabilities which once opened embeds itself into the computer and infects the whole system, eventually disabling it.

COMPUTER HACKING

Such Trojan horses may also be used in order to hack into computers.

One example is the French virus PrettyPark which sent Microsoft Windows users to a custom Internet Relay Chat (IRC) channel without their knowledge. Once there, personal data ranging from e-mail address lists, operating system preferences and registration numbers, passwords and form data – including stored credit card information – were able to be retrieved by the virus writer from victims' PCs without their knowledge. This was the first known worm with Trojan horse capabilities and a custom IRC channel. The virus is spread when a PC user opens an attached e-mail program file named PrettyPark.EXE. When executed, it may display the Windows 3D pipe screen saver while it creates and sends duplicate files of itself to e-mail addresses listed in the user's internet address book. It runs this routine every thirty seconds, without the user's knowledge. It also connects to the IRC channel while the user surfs the web or reads e-mail on a remote server.

Another method commonly used in hacking IT systems is to use programs disguised as normal code, also dubbed Trojan horses. They lie dormant until activated, when they can create holes in security systems and allow hackers to close down systems, steal information or transfer funds. Malicious applets, Java-based Web programs, are also being more frequently used in computer crime.

Three more examples of security disasters are the following:

– Since targeting a group of hackers known as Global Hell (gH), the FBI has had its Web site repeatedly invaded with the culprits posting the message: "gH is here to stay. No one will stop us."

– A Trojan horse attached itself to an application used in a bank. Every time the application was accessed by a particular user it turned out that funds were transferred to the hackers' account.

– On 4 November 2000, the *Economist* reported that somebody had invaded (even) Microsoft's corporate network and may have seen some of its 'source' code, the secret recipe for its software.

A good explanation of the capability of Trojan horse viruses is made in the following article by Thomas C. Greene from 20 July 200 in *www.theregister.co.uk:*

"Two new exploits run without victims' action

It's been a busy week for software bug hunters. First, users of Microsoft Outlook and Outlook Express will be bitterly disappointed to learn that they are now potential sport of an e-mail exploit which will run automatically, without any action from the victim, a possibility which has been predicted for years while Redmond has persistently ignored it.

Malicious code can be concealed in an e-mail header to trigger a buffer overflow, after which an attacker can include commands which will run as if they had been entered by the victim.

Once that's been accomplished, the sky's the limit in terms of what an imaginative attacker could do to a victim's computer – from viewing or sending files to a remote location, changing system settings, deleting files, uploading and executing Trojans, re-formatting a hard disk – virtually anything is possible.

"Clearly this is a serious vulnerability," Microsoft security program manager Scott Culp, warbled during a telephone interview with the Associated Press on Wednesday. (We told you these guys were brilliant.)

Australian Aaron Drew posted his findings Tuesday to the NTBugTraq mailing list, complete with sample code. South American security outfit USSR Labs had also found the exploit approximately two weeks ago but did not announce it in hopes that Redmond would cobble together a fix first.

Microsoft says the hole will not affect users running Outlook in "corporate and workgroup mode"; only those running it in "Internet-only mode", and home users of Outlook Express, are vulnerable.

Microsoft said the problem is in Internet Explorer, and the company recommends that users upgrade to IE 5.01, Service Pack 1. Internet Explorer 5.5 is safe for all users, except those running Windows 2000, who also need to download IE 5.01 SP1.

Microsoft's security bulletin may be found www.microsoft.com/technet/security/bulletin/fq00–043.asp" t "_new" here, while the service pack can be found www.microsoft.com/windows/ie/download/ie501sp1.htm" t "_new" here.If that wasn't bad enough, the US System Administration, Networking, and Security (SANS) Institute found another Microsoft weakness, this time involving ActiveX controls, which it called "probably the most dangerous programming error in Windows workstation (all varieties – 95, 98, 2000, NT 4.0) that Microsoft has made".

A SANS security alert states that users are vulnerable to a total system compromise when they preview or read an infected e-mail message if they're running any of the affected operating systems and have Microsoft Access 97 or 2000, Internet Explorer 4.0 or higher, including version 5.5 that ships with Windows 2000.

The exploit was first discovered 27 June, but Microsoft requested that SANS not release the details until a fix could be developed.

Users running systems with Outlook, Outlook Express, Eudora, or any mail client which uses Internet Explorer to render HTML documents are also vulnerable to this exploit through e-mail, SANS says.

According to the advisory, an attacker can get into Microsoft Access using ActiveX controls without the victim knowing that it's happening. Malicious code can be written so as to execute before the victim is warned, the Institute explains. Even when the victim has disabled active scripting, the code can run. All Windows systems (Windows 2000, NT 4.0, 98 and 95) are vulnerable if they have the following installed: Microsoft Excel 2000 or PowerPoint 97 or 2000; Internet Explorer 4.0 or higher, including 5.5; Outlook, Outlook Express, Eudora, or any other mail reader that uses IE to render HTML."

It should be noted that computer hacking may well constitute criminal damage. This is suggested by the case of *R* v *Whiteley* [1991] TLR 6 February. In that case a conviction was upheld for damaging property contrary to section 1(1) Criminal Damage Act 1971 when the defendant gained unauthorised access to the Joint Academic Network (JANET) and created and deleted files and caused general havoc with the system. It was held that the alteration of the magnetic particles on the discs and the impairment of their usefulness to the owner were sufficient to constitute damage.

INSTANT MESSAGING AND PEER-TO-PEER SYSTEMS

Two new technologies are already starting to take hold: instant messaging and peer-to-peer systems.

Instant Messaging

The first is instant messaging which allows surfers to chat on-line one-to-one. The most popular program for this at present is ICQ (*www.icq.com*) but it is also provided by many of the ISPs and e-mail providers such as AOL, Hotmail and Yahoos' various forms of Instant Messenger. Clearly, these forms of messaging are not necessarily fully secure and may face similar problems to that associated with e-mail including the possibility in the future of catching viruses.

Peer-to-peer systems

These are explained in Chapter 8 (above). Their significance in the present context is that they potentially allow open up huge roads into people's computer systems which are open to abuse through the use of standard viruses and Trojan horses.

SAFER SURFING

Virus protection software

There are a number of products which can help to protect against many viruses. These work a little like a flu jab. They can protect against known strains but not necessarily against new ones which have just been developed. However, with some packages it is possible to up-date one's virus protection daily and this will probably become more popular in the future.

When assessing anti-virus software, users should be careful not just to look at technology performance on a particular platform. The supplier's research capacity should also be analysed.

Practice

Delete doubtful mail

What is clear however is that the best way to be safe is only to open e-mails where the sender is known and it is not a forward from someone else.

Avoid unknown web-sites

Surfers should be aware that they are more likely to pick up bugs when surfing in unsafe waters. The child protection barriers offered by ISPs such as AOL could also be seen in this context as shark nets protecting not only against the excesses in terms of content but also against many of the viruses on the web.

Keep data away from hackers

Further, the best way to store data is in systems which are wholly unconnected with those which are on-line. In any other circumstances there is the possibility that the data may potentially be accessed by hackers.

Reaction time

Reaction time is the key in a virus attack. Companies should produce a protocol so that different IT units know how to escalate the business's response. The Melissa virus spread so fast through corporate IT systems and wreaking havoc that it prompted the FBI to issue its first virus warning.

Back up all data

This is absolutely crucial and should be done regularly. Different methods will probably apply in different circumstances. For the odd word document, floppy discs may still suffice. For larger files, ZIP drives are now affordable and can now carry up to 250 megabytes on each disc. CD writers can burn as much as 650 megabytes of information onto a single disc and so stretch even further. Finally, tapes can match the largest hard discs in terms of capacity.

Passwords

The use of passwords can also help to a limited degree. See in particular 'Is Your Computer Data Safe?' by Mark Harris, *Counsel Magazine*, October 2000, pages 38–41. These can range from Windows passwords, to screen-saver passwords and even file passwords.

These are limited however by the fact that there are often 'backdoors' and 'crack' programs can be freely downloaded off the internet.

'BIOS' passwords are provided by many computers. Effectively these mean that the user has to press a number of keys or combination of keys before the computer will even start up.

Encryption

This is the safest method of transferring data and effectively scrambles the data as soon as it is sent and required a password at the other end in order to unscramble it.

The most popular model at the moment is PGP (Pretty Good Privacy) which is available as a free download (though not for commercial use) at *www.pgpi.com* and may well end up being the industry standard for private e-mails.

Commercial licensed versions of PGP which are functionally identical are available from Network Associates at *www.pgpinternational.com*.

A commercial program which claims to even allows for instant messaging and real-time chat sessions to be held in a secure, encrypted environment is SST (Secure Shuttle Transport).

CHAPTER 11
DATA PROTECTION

"If I say it's safe to surf, it's safe to surf".

Robert Duvall, 'Apocalypse Now'

INTRODUCTION

The statutes relating to data protection set rules for the processing of personal information which is held on computers. E-mail is yet another facility for the transmission of data provided by computers and inevitably will attract the attention of the regulatory framework.

The Data Protection Act 1998 ("the Act") is by far the most important legislative measure in this field. The Act gives individuals certain rights and also lays down a requirement on all those who record and use personal information to do so fairly. Generally those that hold such information are known as data controllers. The people whose information they hold are commonly referred to as data subjects.

Information is a powerful commodity and as such must be protected from abuse. What with the increasing importance of privacy coupled with the growing ease of recording, sending and disseminating information, this area of law takes up a central place in the resolution of the conflicting interests.

This chapter sets out an introduction to these issues.

THE DATA PROTECTION ACT 1998

The Act came into force on 1st March 2000. It repeals the 1984 Act of the same name, though some transitional provisions mean that processing carried out before 24th October 1998 will still be subject to the 1984 Act until October 2001.

Data means information which is being, or will be, processed by a computer. It can also include manual records, but that is not relevant to this work and not considered further. The definition is wide and encompassing. The Act pro-tects "personal data". It is defined as data which relates to a living individual who can be identified from the data and other information which the data controller has, or is likely to have at some future stage, in his possession.

The Act is built around eight principles. The principles are the bedrock of the legislation and are as follows:

The data must be:

(a) fairly and lawfully processed;

(b) processed for limited purposes;

(c) adequate, relevant and not excessive;

(d) accurate;

(e) not kept for longer than is necessary;

(f) processed in line with your rights;

(g) secure; and,

(h) not transferred to countries without adequate protection.

Fairly and lawfully processed

The data must not only be fairly and lawfully processed, but it must also have one of the conditions set out in Schedule 2 of the Act. In order to be lawful "a data user must comply with all the relevant rules of law, whether derived from statute or common law" (see Data Protection Registrar's Guideline 4, *The Data Protection Principles* (third series, November 1994, section 1.6). The conditions set out in Schedule 2 are as follows:

(i)   consent of the subject (silence does not generally amount to effective consent: see *British Gas Trading Ltd* v *Data Protection Registrar* (unreported 24 March 1998), where the failure to return a form indicating that the customer did not want their own details disseminated to others, did not amount to consent. Consent can however, be implied where the use is obvious. See also Data Protection Registrar, *An Introduction to the Data Protection Act 1998*, chapter 3 section 1.6);

(ii) that the processing is necessary for the pursuance of a contract to which the subject is a party, or at the subject's behest in such pursuance;

(iii) pursuant to a legal obligation;

(iv) the processing is necessary in order to protect the vital interests of the subject;

(v) the processing is necessary for the administration of justice or some other public function;

(vi) necessary for the pursuance of legitimate interests, except where the processing is unwarranted by reason of prejudice to the rights and freedoms of the subject.

Where the information is obtained the controller must probably inform the subject as to certain matters so that the subject can decide whether or not to provide the information. The most obvious will be obviously why they want the information. Where the information is not obtained from the subject direct, the controller is not obliged to give the information where the giving of such would be disproportionate or required under a no-contractual legal obligation (see The Data Protection (Conditions Under Paragraph 3 of Part II of Schedule 1) Order 1999 (SI 185/2000).

In determining what is fair it seems to be the law that the fairness is to be assessed in relation to the data subject. The usefulness of the information to the data user is outweighed in such an analysis: see *CCN Systems Ltd* v *Data Protection Registrar* DA/9025/49/9.

Processed for limited purposes

This requirement is simple: it must be obtained for a purpose which is permitted. The processing of information obtained for one legitimate purpose in execution of a non legitimate purpose will not be permitted.

Adequate, relevant and not excessive

The controller is bound not to hold, therefore, information of irrelevance or excessive amounts of information. The processing of such information needs, therefore, to be regulated by all controllers. The ease with which data can be transferred and stored makes it all the more important for controllers to regulate e-mails, and the use of intra/inter-net facilities.

Accurate

This is not to be judged statically – what was once true and accurate may change and the duty upon controllers to ascertain accuracy is a continuing one. Controllers must, therefore, have some means of updating their system.

Not kept for longer than is necessary

What amounts to being longer than necessary, will no doubt depend upon the facts of the case. It is submitted that "necessary" will not be strictly construed where there is a large volume of data and the updating process is undertaken at reasonable intervals.

Processed in line with the subject's rights

This matter is considered in more detail below. In essence the controller will offend this principle unless complying with each right as set out in the Act.

Secure

This principle effectively puts an obligation upon controllers to take appropriate technical and organisational measures against unlawful or unauthorised processing of personal data and against accidental loss or destruction of, or damage to, personal data. The assessment of "appropriate" will no doubt depend upon the organisation concerned and the information in question.

Not transferred to countries without adequate protection

This places a restriction on the transferral of information to countries within the European Economic Area, unless the country concerned ensures an adequate level of protection for the rights and freedoms of data subjects to the processing of such information. The principle will not apply in limited circumstances (e.g. with the subject's consent, or when it is in the public interest: see Schedule 4 of the Act).

This principle will have obvious implications for the use of the internet and e-mail whereby the world is at the touch of a button.

Procedural Protection

The Act requires controllers to register with the Data Protection Commissioner. If no such registration takes place then there is a prohibition on the processing of information: section 17. This prohibition will not apply where it can be shown that

(i)   the manual data was processed as part of a relevant filing system or accessible record;
(ii) where the data has been exempted by the Secretary of State; or
(iii) where the processing is for the *sole* purpose of maintaining a public register.

The Data Protection Commissioner has a general duty to promote good practice: see section 51(1). "Good practice" is defined widely and extends beyond mere compliance with the Act: see section 51(9). This is facilitated by the power to create and enforce codes of practice. The Commissioner has investigation powers in order to judge a controller's compliance with the Act including information notices and warrants of arrest and seizure. The Commissioner can also issue enforcement notices setting out the existing breach and what needs to be done to remedy the same. Failure to do so will lead to the commission of an offence.

Acquired Rights

Data subjects have an entitlement, by section 7, to be informed by any data controller as to whether their personal data is being processed (section 7(1)(a)). Subjects also have a right to receive communication of the personal data, the purpose of processing the same and to whom, in an "intelligible form" (section 7(1)(c)).

Where a decision has been taken by an automated process, the subject has the right to be informed of the logic involved in any such decision (section 7(1)(d)), so long as such logic is not a trade secret in itself (section 8(5)). These rights, together, are known as the "right of subject access". A fee may be chargeable (of a nominal nature) and replies should be made within 40 days or so (see the data protection website: *www.dataprotection.gov.uk*).

A problem thrown up by these rights is the fact that disclosure of information will often include disclosing other data which is personal to other individuals. The Act has made provision for the same in section 7(4)(5)(6) and section 8. The duty upon controllers is not to disclose such information unless the person concerned consents, or, the disclosure is reasonable in all the circumstances. If the controller can disclose the information whilst maintaining confidentiality (e.g. by redaction), the duty to disclose continues.

The subject can also object to the processing taking place at all. The subject must show compelling legitimate grounds. This has been defined in the Act to mean: (a) substantial damage or distress to the subject or to another; *and* (b) that such damage is unwarranted (see section 10(1)). In default of an agreement, the subject can apply for relief from the court. Similar rights exist to prevent the controller from persisting in using the subject's information for direct marketing (see section 11(1)).

Importantly, section 12 provides that a subject has the right to object to any decision, which will significantly affect the subject, being solely taken by any automated process. In the absence of any objection being conveyed to the controller, there still exists upon the controller a duty to notify the subject communicating the fact that the decision was taken by an automated process and allow them an opportunity to reconsider the decision. In a rather convoluted set of particulars the Act provides that this right of notification does not apply where:

   (i)   the Secretary of State has granted exemption;
  (ii) where the decision is taken in the course of steps taken – for the purpose of considering whether to enter into a contract with the subject, or with a view to entering into such a contract, or in the course of performing such a contract;
 (iii) where there is authorisation under an enactment;

    (iv) where the effect of the decision is to grant a request of the subject;
          or,

    (v) steps have been taken to safeguard the legitimate interests of the
        subject.

    (see section 12 (6)(7)).

REMEDIES AND DEFENCES

Section 12 of the Act allows recovery of compensation from the controller if an individual suffers damage by reason of any contravention of any of the requirements of the Act. The Act also provides that compensation for distress may be payable where the individual has suffered the distress along with damage, or distress alone whereby the contravention related to the processing of personal data for "special purposes" (i.e. for the purposes of journalism, art, or literary work).

It shall be a defence for the controller to prove that he had taken such care as in all the circumstances was reasonably required to comply with the requirement concerned: section 13(3).

There are certain classified exemptions to the right to view material. Some of these have been considered above. In addition, where the disclosure of the information would be likely to affect:

    (a) the way crime is detected or prevented;

    (b) catching or prosecuting offenders;

    (c) assessing or collecting taxes or duty;

that information will also be exempt.

Further, under certain circumstances, your right to see research, and certain health and social work details, may also be limited.

Personal data processed only for special purposes (i.e. art, journalistic, or literary works) are exempt if the processing is undertaken with a view to publication, that publication is in the public interest and that compliance with the provisions of the Act is incompatible with the special purposes (see section 32). This reflects the increasing importance of the freedom of expression as guaranteed by the Human Rights Act 1998.

An individual can seek enforcement for compensation through the courts or refer the matter to the Commissioner. The Commissioner can take enforcement action against a data controller. The controller has a right to appeal to the independent Data Protection Tribunal. If the Tribunal upholds the

Commissioner's decision and the data controller continues to breach the principles, it may amount to a criminal offence. This could then be prosecuted by the Commissioner.

E-MAILS AS PERSONAL DATA

As stated above, personal data is data which relates to a living individual who can be identified from the data and other information which the data controller has, or is likely to have at some future stage, in his possession. It is suggested that the requirement for identification is all important. Is an e-mail address therefore personal data?

At first blush this seems incredulous. However, *paulmcgrath@acompany.co.uk* gives the receiving party the following information:

(1) the full name of the sender,

(2) the company that the sender works for,

(3) that it is a UK based company.

The contents of the e-mail may well be personal and may well give even more indicia as to the sender's identity and location.

The Directive (95/46 [1995] O.J. 1281/31) states that account should be taken of all the means likely reasonably to be used to identify the person either directly or indirectly (see recital 26 and Article 2(a)). Therefore it is arguable that many e-mails are personal data which are processed by those who receive them. If that is the case, e-mail users may have to register.

The implications of this are obviously quite wide. The processing of the data must be in accordance with the eight principles outlined above and should not be stored longer than "necessary" (the 5th principle). This gives rise to questions as to the storing or deleting of messages / addresses on the e-mail system. Personal e-mails received at work, if personal data, must be kept "secure" and secret (the 7th principle) and yet as we have seen, employers may have a right to impose surveillance and to read e-mails. "Cookies" which store user's preferences also may attract the attention of the legislation.

In Germany, e-mail addresses are viewed as personal data. However, to create some balance, German law also generally requires service providers to offer anonymous e-mail addresses.

For a more detailed analysis of this subject see the illustrative article by Justin Harrington, *Ent. LR*, Issue 7, 2000, page 141.

OTHER RELEVANT PROVISIONS

Of particular interest in recent times is the E-Commerce Directive. Of relevance to data protection is the section relating to commercial communications. This generally means direct marketing. There are various requirements that must be complied with. The communication must identify itself as an advertisement, the identity of the person noting the communication must be clearly shown and any advertisement or promotion offering competitions or gifts must be identifiable as such and also promoted in a clear and unequivocal way.

In the UK the Electronic Communications Act 2000 allows the industry to take voluntary measures to regulate unsolicited e-mails.

The Telecommunications (Data, Protection and Privacy) Regulations 1999 apply to all publicly available telecommunications systems. Internal e-mail will not therefore be covered. It is not clear to what extent the Regulations apply to e-mail generally. The DTI had previously indicated that e-mails would not be covered and this receives some support from the use of the words "calls" in the original Telecoms Directive 97/66. However, it was indicated by the Registrar (the former title for the Commissioner) that e-mails would be covered.

The Regulations impose standards on all direct marketing (and not just the equivalent of "cold calling") and generally state when unsolicited marketing can take place and the prohibitions on the same. For further information see the *Encyclopedia of Information Technology Law* 16–641 – 16–659 inclusive.

EU DRAFT DIRECTIVE

On 12 July 2000 the European Commission published a Draft Directive on Personal Data and Protection of Privacy regarding Electronic Communications. This is intended to replace the 1997 Directive (97/66/EC), adapting and updating the existing provisions to new and future developments in electronic communications services and technologies.

The main changes are to replace the definitions of telecommunications networks and services with electronic communications services in order to ensure the coverage of all types of transmission services, regardless of the technology used, and to add new definitions of calls, communications traffic data and location data.

These changes are intended to make the legislation technology neutral, for example by replacing the phrase "to establish a call" with the phrase "the transmission of a communication", and include a provision proposing that location data giving the geographic position of mobile users should not be used without the consent of the subscriber except with regard to the emergency services and under existing derogations concerning public and national security.

Amendments are proposed to measures concerning directories of subscribers to take into account that consumers subscribing to mobile telephones or email, for example, do not usually register this information in public directories in the same way as most land lines are registered. It is therefore proposed that subscribers be given the right to determine whether they are listed in a public directory and with which of their personal data.

Measures in Directive 97/66/EC currently provide protection against unsolicited calls, but this has only been applied to voice telephony. It is proposed that these measures be extended to cover electronic mail for direct marketing purposes other than at the request of a subscriber (spam), with the same type of protection as exists for faxes, prohibiting spamming except for those subscribers who have indicated they want to receive such communications.

The Commission noted that such a harmonised system for this would be more effective, since e-mail addresses often give no indication of country of origin. It was proposed that Member States transpose the provisions of this draft Directive by 31 December 2001.

EU/US CO-OPERATION

On 1 November 2000 the US Commerce Department introduced the U.S.-EU safe harbor privacy framework. US organisations may sign up to this which enables them to comply with EU privacy rules. The new website is *www.export.gov/safeharbor.*

The framework was developed by the Department of Commerce, in consultation with the European Commission, industry and non-governmental organizations to provide U.S. organizations with a practical means of satisfying the "adequacy" requirement under the European Directive on Data Protection. The safe harbour was officially recognized by the EU in Summer 2000 as a basis of protecting European citizens' privacy.

For U.S. companies, it offers a way to avoid experiencing interruptions in their business dealings with the EU or facing prosecution by European authorities under European privacy laws.

U.S. companies can access the web site to learn about the safe harbor framework, read the actual agreement, evaluate their needs, and sign up online.

EU organizations, in turn, can ensure that they are sending information to a U.S. organization participating in the safe harbour by viewing the on-line list of safe harbour organizations posted on the website. The list will contain the names of all U.S. companies that have committed to the safe harbour framework.

(For US government e-commerce policy generally see *www.ecommerce.gov*).

TECHNICAL PROFICIENCY

An article by Lucy Sherriff in *www.theregister.co.uk* on 13 July 2000 highlights the need for companies holding personal data to ensure that all of their systems are technically proficient:

"Hotmail punts user email addresses to advertisers

A glitch in the code at Hotmail has resulted in subscribers' email addresses being sent to online advertisers, the company conceded yesterday. This is not a problem unique to the Microsoft site, but it is the latest in a string of embarrassing technical problems for the free emailer. The problem is this: when users open HTML newsletters containing banner ads, a phenomenon known as "data spill" occurs. In order for the company responsible for the banner ad to know where to send its data, opening the newsletter automatically sends the recipients email address and personal data back to the advertiser. In a statement to *The Register,* Microsoft said that to the best of its knowledge no consumer email had been abused by this error. Microsoft was spared this further ignominy by the moral conduct of the advertising companies, however unlikely that may sound. DoubleClick, for example, automatically truncates personal information accompanying a referrer URL. "Microsoft places the highest priority on consumer privacy and security," the red-faced company said. "As soon as we were made aware of the error the Hotmail team began work to fix it. It is a common problem on the net, and we expect to have it fixed by August." Experts estimate that the site has had the problem for about six months, and that about one million addresses were compromised."

USEFUL CONTACTS

The postal address of the Data Protection Commissioner is:

Wycliffe House,
Water Lane,
Wilmslow,
Cheshire SK9 5AF.

The web-site is *www.dataprotection.gov.uk* and the e-mail address is *mail@dataprotection.gov.uk*.

The information line is 01625 545745.

Data controllers who want to notify should call 01625 545740, though this can be accomplished online.

CHAPTER 12
MULTI-MEDIA, BROADCASTING AND TELECOMMUNICATIONS

INTRODUCTION

The internet has blown open the opportunity to broadcast images and sounds to a new market with new capabilities. The laws and regulatory bodies have hitherto not had to deal with such a massive undertaking as providing for the multiplicity of possibilities created by the internet. The development in this area will be fast moving and no doubt statutory regulation will become more and more difficult meaning that Codes of Practice and case law may well take the front seat in developing the current law. This chapter aims to identify the major issues in this speedily adapting environment.

THE CURRENT POSITION

At present there are regulatory bodies to control telecommunications and broadcasting. Telecommunications is historically concerned with the infrastructure for the transmission of information, whereas broadcasting has been historically concerned with the final product as delivered to the viewers. The principal difference also relates to the medium of communication: cables and wireless telegraphy. The two principal statutes are the Broadcasting Act 1990 and the Telecommunications Act 1984.

The Broadcasting Act 1990 provides and regulates independent television and sound programmes provided on television or radio frequencies. Digital forms of television were recognised and provided for in the Broadcasting Act 1996 including the provision, by the ITC, of licences to provide multiplex services. The Secretary of State must keep under review the extent of multiplexing for the purpose of considering how long it would be appropriate for television broadcasting services to continue to be provided in analogue form (section 33).

The Telecommunications Act 1984 provides a similar sphere of regulation and licensing and made provision for the non-exclusivity of the telecommunications system. The Act also set up the Director of Telecommunications and the department, known as OFTEL.

The Director and OFTEL were set up to issue licences and to regulate the operators.

The government had to amend UK licences in order to bring them in line with the EC Directive (Directive 97/13/EC on a Common Framework for General Authorisations and Individual Licences in the Field of Telecommunications Services ('Licensing Directive')), which aimed to produce a common framework for licensing.

REGULATION AND THE FUTURE

Internet Service Providers are not directly regulated, but that is not to say that they do not have a serious interest in the approach to regulation. The availability and cost of telecommunications access, and the proportion which the ISP receives, are all very important. In this regard the telecommunications company are regulated to allow freedom of competition.

The benefit of the internet in relation to voice transmission is that long distance calls can be made at the cost of a local rate. As the internet interacts more and more with existing, and regulated, mediums of communication so it gets closer to being regulated itself. The Electronic Communications Act 2000 provides for the self regulation of cryptography service providers, and the possibility of a statutory scheme should the self regulation fail. The "tScheme" (the self regulation) should be operational by the time this work is published. The scheme will set the minimum standards expected. Part III of the Act simplifies the amendment to telecommunications licences.

Both statutory schemes now face a new challenge – the internet and multimedia.

Media and the internet were always heading for some kind of unison. The internet represents choice to a vast audience. As the technology moves on so does the public expectation as to when and how they view the information. It was not so long ago that the capability of watching video-recorded programmes was seen as a luxury. However, now we are moving more towards a society unfettered by broadcasting timing where instead people will take information when they want it, and will view it when they want to. Such an example of the push towards this is the increasing development of "multiplexing" (i.e. multiple channels with multiple screening of material to allow increased choice).

It is the coalition between digital television and the internet which has given rise to the term "convergence" (see further, Command Paper: Regulating Communications: Approaching Convergence in the Information Age 1997–98). The internet is increasingly becoming a broadcast medium. Internet access will no doubt increase in the home through the television itself along with additional minimal hardware.

Much like the increase in the amount of web-sites, there is likely to be an increase in the use of broadcasting. This is not just in the media sense but also in advertising and corporate matters. This obviously brings with it issues such as copyright (see Chapter 8) whereby encryption may be the answer to help regulate the use of protected material.

The regulation of content is made all the more difficult as the mediums which are being used are different. There is, on the one hand, television pictures (traditionally received from the air rather than a cable) and telecommunications. Both have their own regulatory bodies. This will have to change if it is to maintain true effectiveness. Such changes are themselves hot topics of debate. Given that the Prime Minister has recently indicated that he wishes the UK to be a world leader in internet technology, such issues must be resolved with an extensive consultation process to ensure that the best solution is arrived at.

In its White Paper regarding the future of regulation entitled 'A New Future for Communications' (*www.communicationswhitepaper.gov.uk*) which was published towards the end of 2000, the government refers to the UK becoming "the most dynamic and competitive communications and media market in the world". As part of that transformation, the White Paper proposes a cross-industry multi-media watchdog, the Office of Communications (Ofcom), which would be a merger of the Office of Telecommunications (Oftel), the Radio Authority, the Independent Television Commission (ITC) and other bodies.

As Nigel Powell reported in *The Times* on 22 January 2001:

> "The new body will use its powers to govern competition and compliance of these industries, working with the Office of Fair Trading. It will ensure that new technologies such as electronic programme guides and the allocation of future spectrum will be implemented fairly. The moves have been prompted by the growing convergence of technologies and markets. The consumer is being offered similar services on differing platforms, be it internet access via the television, radio programming via the World Wide Web or games on a mobile phone."

An immediate issue which would face any such regulator is the increased worry over the proliferation of obscene video recordings / images which will inevitably come with the increased technology (see Chapter 5, above).

COMPETITION

The Competition Act 1998 was passed to reflect the provisions of Articles 85 and 86 of the E.C. Treaty. The Act seeks to prevent firstly agreements and practices which stifle or restrict competition which may affect trade in the UK; and secondly the abuse of one or more undertakings of a dominant position in a market which may affect trade in the UK. The Act, it is suggested, will be hard pressed to regulate and provide adequate cover for digital media, which is more in the cast of a medium rather than a market, but which has a fundamentally important position in success or failure of ventures.

The providers of digital services are wide ranging and there will be problems in identifying a true abuse of a dominant position. The requirements in finding an abuse of a dominant position may provide little protection against multilateral action from a number of small, but crucial, service providers.

This position is not to be assisted by the lack, at present, of any specified regulatory body equipped with the material and resources to identify problems and to eliminate them. This is likely to be an extremely difficult exercise given the amount of sources producing the material which is being shown and the vast, and international, audience. Self regulation may be the key in this fast changing technological area.

CONCLUSION

The future of internet regulation is sure to be fast changing. There is a need for sensible and proportionate regulation and no doubt the age old debate between freedom of information / expression and that of censorship will be at the centre of any developments.

CHAPTER 13
PROFESSIONAL CONDUCT

INTRODUCTION

The internet has created a global market-place not only for the sale of goods but also for the provision of services by qualified professionals such as accountants, architects engineers, medics, teachers, religious professionals, chartered surveyors and lawyers.

This issue of negligence and by implication professional negligence was dealt with in Chapter 7 above. However, even issues which do not amount to negligence may amount to professional misconduct.

Clearly, each profession's rules are different and peculiar to that profession. It is not intended in this chapter to provide a comprehensive guide to each of these set of rules. Instead, it sets out some of the issues of which those practising professionals should be aware when either practising on-line or by e-mail. These are in addition to the issues raised throughout the rest of this book.

It is hoped that each profession's Code of Conduct will continue to be updated in the light of technological and legal developments which impinge on this area in order to clarify any doubts which may exist. In the meantime and in the absence of such guidance, the keyword should be caution.

CONFIDENTIALITY

Most professions have some form of rule with regard to confidentiality. This may take two forms: as to the identification of the client and as to information passed on by the client.

Identification of client

The fact that a firm has approached a particular accountancy firm or management consultancy may be commercially sensitive in itself. For this reason, some professions protect the identity of the professional's client.

In such a situation, these professionals must be careful when sending block e-mails. Some e-mail providers allow people to send a block e-mail with recipients only seeing their name under the heading of addressee.

Attention in this regard must also be paid to the data protection issues which are dealt with in other parts of this book. In particular, avoiding giving away not only one's client list but also potentially their e-mail addresses.

Client confidence

Correspondence between the professional and the client is likely to be confidential. This question foxed American legal ethics committees in the mid-1990s. Some judges were of the view that e-mails were no safer than sending information on a post-card. Others were of the view that it was wholly secure.

The truth is probably something in the middle. First, e-mails may be intercepted at any of the nodes through which they must pass on the way to their destination. Second, as with the post or faxes, they may be misdirected. It is probably not very far from the truth to use the analogies of fax or standard mail services. At present, these methods suffice for professional communications and there is no reason to suggest that e-mails would not do as well.

However, encryption may sometimes be appropriate depending upon the sensitivity of the information. An analogy may be that sort of information which can only be sent by recorded delivery or even by hand.

This is effectively the standard that the Bar Council arrived at in its Practice Standards in 1997. For an analysis of the arguments at the time see article in *Counsel* magazine, January/February 1997, 'Barristers Don't Surf' by Nick Critelli and Tim Kevan.

On 7 October 1998, the *Law Society Gazette* stated (at page 39) that:

> "As with any method of communication, you should consider the confidentiality aspects of using e-mails and the Internet and take whatever measures are reasonably necessary to ensure client confidentiality. It may not, in some circumstances be appropriate to use these forms of communications."

In Bar News, December 2000, the Bar Council issued a Guidance Note on E-Mail Security and emphasised that "E-mail is not completely secure". It continues:

> "The possibility cannot be excluded that the Courts will impose liability upon professionals for negligence for losses arising out of the sending of e-mails of confidential, commercially or litigation sensitive, or privileged communication in an unencrypted or unprotected form

which are misdirected or published to the disadvantage of the owner or intended recipient. Liability may be imposed more readily if the systems for encryption are free, or inexpensive, and readily available."

It also suggests the use of a tracking system to ensure delivery to the correct address, care in clicking and regular up-dating of virus checking.

Finally, it states that it is likely to be sensible to include as a matter of course in all e-mail communications a confidentiality/privacy/privilege notice at the top of the e-mail as appears in faxes. It gives the following as an example of such a notice:

"From: A. Barrister
         Address
         Phone and Fax numbers
To: [Name and address of recipient]

                Privacy and Confidentiality Notice
This message is confidential and intended solely for the person to whom it is address. It may contain privileged and confidential information. If you are not the intended recipient you must not read, copy, distribute, discuss or take any action in reliance on it. If you have received this information in error, please notify me or my clerk as soon as possible on the above telephone number. Thank you."

DUTY TO CHECK MAIL BOX

If a professional uses and advertises an e-mail address, he may also have a duty to check his e-mail box just as he may have a duty to keep a regular check over snail mail which arrives at his registered address. Certainly, it would be advisable to do so. It will become all the more so as professionals receive instructions to act by e-mail (See article in *Counsel* magazine, January/February 1997 'Barristers Don't Surf' by Nick Critelli and Tim Kevan).

ON-LINE ADVICE

This may be provided in a number of ways but in particular, by e-mail and through notice-boards and as well as the negligence issues raised in Chapter 7, may also present various professional conduct issues.

E-mail

Advice provided by e-mail will usually be specific to the addressee. There may be problems in this regard for some professions if there has not been a face to face meeting. For example, doctors diagnosing without a physical examination may be open to some criticism. However, this will probably constitute preliminary advice similar to that provided over the telephone at present.

Another problem in this regard may arise from the need for a retainer. Some professions insist upon the client signing a retainer or other form of formal instruction before any work is done. If this is the case then there may be problems for those that simply reply to an e-mail from a new client who has not signed such a document. Clarification should be sought with the professional body as to whether a retainer may be signed by e-mail. In principle, there is no reason why not. If this suffices, then the retainer may be sent by e-mail and once this has been returned, work may be commenced.

A final problem in this regard arises where the person asking advice has not fully identified themselves. If the professional does not know who he is advising all sorts of problems can arise. An immediate one is that a potential conflict of interest may arise if he is already advising a competitor of the person now asking for advice.

The issue here will probably boil down to how specific is the information demanded and provided. Lawyers, for example, can write articles and books setting out the law as it stands and giving their points on view on the issues in dispute. What they cannot do is to give away confidential information obtained from one of their clients.

Notice-boards

Advice provided in reply to a question which has been posted on a notice board or in a chat room on the internet is likely to exacerbate any problems suggested above with regard to e-mail. In particular, the recipient of the advice is much more likely to be anonymous.

It is unlikely to help the giver of advice that he was also acting in an anonymous capacity although it may be of some significance that he was not acting in a professional capacity.

DIRECT MARKETING AND ADVERTISING

Some professions have restrictions on direct marketing and advertising and in this respect should clarify the position with regard to block e-mails and on-line advertising through for example, having web-site addresses on another web-site in one form or another.

On 7 October 1998, the *Law Society Gazette* stated (at page 39) that although [at that time] the Law Society's view was effectively that the Business Names Act did not apply to e-mails (for which see the next Chapter):

> "The contents of e-mails and Internet messages could make them subject to the Solicitors Publicity Code, however, if they promote your firm."

INTERACTIVE SELF-HELP GUIDES

Ultimately, guides will develop, on CD Rom, DVD or on-line that provide advice to generic problems usually the subject of professional advice. For example, a user may type in answers to various questions and an answer may automatically appear in response. Alternatively, this may be done through the filling out of a form which is sent by e-mail and automatically responded to.

The professional conduct question in this regard is whether automated responses should be put in the same category as a self-help book which directs the reader to generic answers which have already been written or whether it would constitute professional advice. The former would seem the more appropriate but it remains to be seen how professional bodies will deal with this question.

DIRECT ACCESS

Some professions, such as barristers, are limited as to who they may accept instructions from. Traditionally, barristers were only able to accept instructions from solicitors although this has been widened somewhat in recent years.

However, it remains the case that they may not accept instructions direct from a member of the general public. Therefore, there may be extra complications for these professionals with regard to advising by e-mail or on noticeboards, for example.

In *Bar News* in June 2000, it was reported that Professional Standards Committee had considered whether counsel could properly accept instructions through an internet company where the company acted as an introducer between solicitor and counsel. They agreed to investigate the situation in more detail before taking a final decision.

PHARMACISTS

Ordering of drugs on-line

Some on-line health organisations may ask questions of the customer and then provide them with certain drugs. Issues immediately arise as to where the sale takes place, whether it is licensed within the premises or even whether it is legal within the particular jurisdiction. (See article by Laurence C. Kennedy in *Computers and Law*, August/September 2000, pages 31–34 on Medicine, Law and the Internet.)

Prescriptions by e-mail

Savings in both time and money may be made if drugs which have been prescribed may be ordered by e-mail. However, when prescriptions are received the pharmacist has a duty to ensure they are genuine. Further, prescription medicine can only be issued where the principal prescription is present or where the pharmacist knows that it is going to be received. Therefore, at present, it does not appear that e-mailed prescriptions would suffice. However, in the future a system may be developed which may allow prescriptions to be made by e-mail. The electronic signatures referred to in the Communications Act 2000 may well be able to be utilised in this regard.

CHAPTER 14
VICARIOUS LIABILITY

INTRODUCTION

One of the greatest risks for employers is their potential liability for the actions of their employees. This chapter sets out an introduction to the law in this area.

TORT

The classic statement of vicarious liability was made, and has been constantly approved, in *Salmon on Tort*. This is recorded in the 18th edition as follows:

> "It is clear that the master is responsible for acts actually authorised by him: for liability would exist in this case, even if the relation between the parties was merely one of agency, and not one of service at all. But a master, as opposed to the employer of an independent contract, is liable even for acts which he has authorised that nay rightly be regarded as modes – although improper modes – of doing them. In other words, a master is responsible not merely for what he authorises his servant to do, but also for the way in which he does it. If a servant does negligently that which he was authorised to do carefully, or if he does fraudulently that which he was authorised to do honestly, or if he does mistakenly that which he was authorised to do correctly, his master will answer for that negligence, fraud or mistake. On the other hand, if the unauthorised and wrongful act of the servant is not so connected with the authorised act as to be a mode of doing it, but is an independent act, the master is not responsible: for in such a case the servant is not acting in the course of his employment, but has gone outside of it."

This has, for most part, been applied in all situations whereby course of employment / master – servant is in issue. Importantly, this is not the case for discrimination (see below). There must usually be some element of control in some form or fashion. In determining the status of an employee, the courts will look at all the relevant factors concerned and will not be swayed materially by what the parties have intended or labelled their relationship as: see *Ferguson* v *Dawson Partners (Contractors) Ltd* [1976] 1 WLR 1213.

There are various tests for establishing employment, but in essence all factors need to be appraised and the court need to make a qualitative assessment of the true nature of the position.

Whether something is or is not in the course of employment may well hinge upon whether there has been any prohibition upon the activity in question. For instance in *C.P.R.* v *Lockhart* [1942] A.C. 591 an employee was authorised to use his own car in the course of his employment provided that it was insured. The employee had an accident and his car was uninsured. It was held that the company were vicariously liable as the mode of employment was permitted, it was only the way in which he carried out that mode of employment which caused the problem. Contrast this with where the class of acts concerned are prohibited. For instance in *Iqbal* v *London Transport Executive* (1973) 16 K.I.R. 39 a bus conductor was expressly forbidden to drive buses. When told to get an engineer to move a bus, and instead he did it himself resulting in a tort, the bus company were not held vicariously liable – driving buses was not in the course of his employment.

EXAMPLE

Multi-national shooting and fishing company Tim Rose Country Sports PLC employ champion mountain-biker Abigail Good in a part-time standard data-entering job, in particular for up-dating the records of their customers. Her computer is only networked for data entry and she is forbidden to use other machines to access the internet. However, Abigail Good uses an empty work station and accesses the e-mail. She sends a defamatory e-mail to Asa Brebner, an employee of another firm, Glen Hawkins Security Limited. Asa Brebner then sues both Abigail Good and Tim Rose Country Sports Limited.

Tim Rose Country Sports Limited will have a defence if they can show that the action took place outside of Abigail Good's employment. In the present circumstances one of the strongest arguments that they will have is the fact that the activity itself (i.e. the e-mail) was prohibited for that particular worker. It was not in her job at all and she would never need to access it. In those circumstances, they would have a good defence.

Now consider that Abigail Good was an account manager in the sales team and had access to the e-mail and there was no guidance as to its proper use. In these circumstances, Tim Rose Country Sports Limited will find it more difficult to establish that the activity was outside of the course of Abigail Good's employment as the mode of operation was by e-mail and it was simply that the contents that were not.

In order to achieve maximum protection employers must set out in a clear and unambiguous policy (signed by employees to say that it has been read and accepted into their contract of employment) with regard which activities are permitted and which are not and further, which are required by the contract of employment and which will be viewed as extraneous to such a contract. The clearer the policy, the more likelihood there is that employers will evade liability (subject of course to the important qualification that the Court will always be the judge of whether a party is vicariously responsible and will not be bound by contractual principles in this regard).

There is a wide ambit under vicarious liability and employers should be aware that liability is often not too difficult to establish. Perhaps the most effective measure is prevention as opposed to cure. Monitoring and supervision may be the key (see also the chapter relating to employee surveillance).

Where the employment of an independent contractor has taken place, different considerations apply. Generally where an employer has employed an independent contractor of sufficient prima facie competence, then he will not be held responsible for their torts:

> "Unquestionably, no one can be made liable for an act or breach of duty, unless it be traceable to himself or his servant or servants in the course of his or their employment. Consequently, if an independent contractor is employed to do a lawful act, and in the course of the work he or his servants commit some casual act of wrong or negligence, the employer is not answerable"
>
> (per Williams J. *Pickard* v *Smith* (1861) 10 C.B. (N.S.) 470).

There are certain exceptions to this in relation to certain non-delegable duties. In some ways they are practical exceptions only rather than technical exceptions as in reality the employer is more in breach of his own duty rather than accepting responsibility for the breach of another's duty. In any event, these exceptions are unlikely to be of relevance to e-mail or the internet and are not considered further.

THEFT

It had been previously thought that where dishonest actions on the part of employees had taken place, vicarious liability would not be established as it plainly was not in the course of employment. However, this has proved to be incorrect.

It is suggested that the case law in this area establishes that vicarious liability will be shown where it can be shown that the goods/information in question has been entrusted to an employee, and the mere fact that the employment provided the opportunity for a theft to take place is not enough (see for example: *Morris* v *C W Martin & Sons Ltd* [1966] 1 QB 716; *Heasmans (a firm)* v *Clarity Cleaning Co Ltd* [1987] ICR 949; and *Port Swettenham Authority* v *T W Wu & Co* [1979] A.C. 580).

FRAUD

Internet based fraud is on the increase, and therefore employers would be well advised to pay particular attention not only to monitoring such frauds but also the law governing when they may be held liable for the same.

The House of Lords in *Armagas Ltd* v *Mundogas (The Ocean Frost)* [1986] 1 AC 717 stated that there existed a different set of principles than that set out for other aspects of this area. Fraud involves an active deception between the employee and the deceived leading to some benefit to the fraudster. The victim must show that he relied upon the inducement. A decision as to whether an employee has "committed the fraud in the course of his employment can only be made after the authority, actual or ostensible, with which the employee is clothed, has been ascertained" (see *Clerk & Lindsell on Torts*, 18th ed. 5–41). The key for such reasoning is that the third party is directly affected by the apparent authority and acts upon it. In other words the appearance that the employee is acting in the course of his employment is instrumental in the loss and fraud itself (see *Uxbridge Permanent Benefit Building Society* v *Pickard* [1939] 2 KB 248). In this sense the concept of contractual agency comes into play and thus the justification for the peculiar nature of the special rules for fraud is made clearer: "If the agent commits the fraud purporting to act in the course of business such as he was authorised, or held out as authorised, to transact on account of his principal, then the latter may be held liable for it" (see *Lloyd* v *Grace, Smith & Co* [1912] A.C. 716 at 725).

In essence, therefore, employers must be aware that they may be held liable for the fraud of their employees if the fraud arises out of the improper exercise of their ostensible or actual authority. If the employee does not in fact have authority then in order to be liable the employer will have to be found to have induced the victims belief that the employee was in fact acting with authority (see *The Ocean Frost* [1986] A.C. 717; *Credit Lyonnais NV* v *Export Credits Guarantee Dept* [1999] 2 WLR 540).

DISCRIMINATION

An employer will be vicariously liable for discrimination by his employees in the course of their employment (see section 41 Sex Discrimination Act 1975 and the equivalent provision, section 32 Race Relations Act 1976). It shall be a defence for the employer to show that "he took such steps as were reasonably practicable to prevent the employee from doing that act, or from doing in the course of his employment acts of that description" (section 41(3), 32(3) respectively). For employment purposes under the Act it is essential to appreciate that the normal common law meaning of "in the course of employment" are not to be applied (see *Jones* v *Tower Boot Co Ltd* [1997] ICR 254). So for these purposes it has been held that harassment at a leaving party and public house may well amount to "within course of employment" and thus embracing social occasions within the Act's remit (see *Chief Constable of Lincolnshire Police* v *Stubbs* [1999] IRLR 81. It was made clear that a purely social gathering would not however be covered.

Such ratio could have fundamental ramifications for employers in relation to e-mail. E-mails which are deemed to amount to discriminatory harassment which are sent by employees merely at their employment and using the computer terminals may attract liability for their employers. This is particularly likely to be the case with e-mails sent internally within the company where the connection with work is all the more obvious.

In order to establish the defence under section 41(3) or 32(3), above, it has been held that where the employer had no knowledge of the of unlawful discrimination, the employer may have made his defence out if he shows that there was proper and adequate staff supervision and publication by the employers of their equal opportunities policy (see *Balgobin and Francis* v *London Borough of Tower Hamlets* [1987] ICR 829).

The impact that this area of law will have upon the liability for improper use of e-mail will be influenced by the law relating to e-mail surveillance as discussed elsewhere in this work. Where personal e-mails are banned, then the detection of the same can be easily maintained by an IT department. However, this is not the case whereby e-mails are sent within the company for business purposes but include discriminatory matters. How then is the employer to ensure adequate supervision?

There is no easy solution to this matter. It is suggested that employers have a widely available equal opportunities policy, along with a grievance procedure and that it is made clear to all employees that e-mails are for business use only and that personal comments should be omitted or left to basic matters of politeness. This may seem a little drastic and over cautious, however the middle ground is hard to achieve. In terms of supervision, this would be almost impossible given the amount of communication undertaken – it would be comparable to attempting to supervise all telephone conversations between employees. It is suggested that in order to assist with this matter, all employees be informed that they have a duty to forward any e-mails which appear to be discriminatory or offensive to the human resources department, or some other responsible officer. Employees should have it made clear to them that discriminatory e-mails will attract disciplinary sanctions.

Of slightly less significance, is the provision that persons who aid and abet another to commit an unlawful act are themselves deemed to have committed an unlawful act of the like description (section 42(1) or section 33 respectively). An employee can therefore be liable as well as his employer for the same discrimination. Indeed the employer may show that he has a defence under section 41(3) (or 32(3)) leaving only the individual to face liability: see *AM* v *WC and SPV* [1999] IRLR 410. This could well encourage the inclusion of the individual in any legal proceedings.

In relation to course of employment, it may well be more arguable that where the activity in question has been undertaken by use of company equipment (e.g. a company mobile phone), there is scope for saying that this was therefore within the course of employment. This argument may well depend on the factual circumstances involved. However, it is suggested that the provision of the equipment is not, by itself, sufficient to raise a case to answer against the employer and that what truly ought to be assessed is the factual nature of the activity against the test as outlined above.

The employer may be advised to give training on equal opportunities and the proper and legitimate use of mobile 'phones, e-mails and any other technology that they provide for the transmission of communications in, and incidental to, their course of employment.

GENERAL CRIMINAL LAW

Apart from the specific examples given above, it should be appreciated that vicarious responsibility can arise in many situations. The criminal law is mainly aimed at the perpetrators of offences (i.e. the person who directly carries out the offence). It should be noted that generally corporations can be liable just as natural persons can be for most offences (see below).

Aside from corporations, vicarious liability is usually confined to summary offences only and not those on indictment. With absolute offences (i.e. those not requiring any intent or mens rea) the person on whom the duty falls is responsible, whether he has delegated or whether he has acted through a servant. Where some form of mens rea is required, it will usually depend upon the intention of the Act as to whether vicarious liability will exist: see *Mousell Bros Ltd* v *London and North Western Railway Co* [1917] 2 KB 836.

Innocent Agent

Companies who find themselves being unwittingly used in the course of a criminal offence are not likely to share any of the guilt. The reason for this is based in public policy and fairness and the law will seek out and punish the true perpetrator despite the fact certain elements of the crime have been carried out seemingly directly by the innocent agent.

One can be an innocent agent either by incapacity (e.g. infancy), because one lacks the mens rea (e.g. he did not possess any criminal intent) or because one was subject to duress (e.g. violent threats).

In *R* v *Stringer* (1991) 94 Cr App Rep 13 it was held that a business manager who signed false invoices intending for unwitting employees to pass them for payment was guilty as the perpetrator when the employees did so. The employees acting without mens rea would not be guilty of any offence. It is suggested that these principles would apply equally in the field of electronic business and communication. E-mail is simply another means of communication which may facilitate such criminal activity.

Accomplice

A person will be an accomplice and liable to the same charges if it can be shown that the person concerned aided, abetted, counselled or procured the commission of the offence prior to the offence being committed. These offences apply generally to all offences (including inchoate offences, such as attempts, conspiracy, incitement to commit an offence etc).

Aiding and abetting is in relation to the granting of assistance to commit the offence or the incitement and encouragement of the same. Counsel is simply to advise or encourage and adds little to the list. Procurement is shown when the offence is brought about by a person or is caused by a person by steps that he has taken.

Persons can be guilty under these provision for failing to exercise control over the persons concerned (e.g. see *Tuck* v *Robson* [1970] 1 WLR 741).

A person will be guilty as an accomplice if it can be shown that there was an intent to assist, encourage or procure the commission of the offence which is to be committed with necessary mens rea of the perpetrator and with the knowledge of the facts which are required to constitute the offence. Plainly employers merely providing the means (e.g. e-mail and internet facilities) will not be an accomplice merely because the criminal uses these facilities as a tool in committing his offences. However if he knows that his tools, whatever they be, are to be used for the commission of an offence then he may be so guilty – the exact facts do not have to be known.

Aside from various little frequented statutory measures there are two common law exceptions to the fact that some intention is necessary. The employer will still be guilty of an offence if (a) his employee creates a public nuisance on his property or the highway, or (b) his employee commits a defamatory libel unless the employer proves that he did not authorise the publication and that the publication was not due to want of care on his part (see Libel Act 1843 section 7).

Liability of Corporates and Directors

A corporate can be held criminally liable as a natural person can be. The scope is obviously slightly more limited in practice than in theory.

There are various explicit corporate offences which are set out by statute. References to person in a statutory offence includes a corporation unless the contrary intention appears: see section 5, Schedule 1 Interpretation Act 1978. Guilt on the part of a corporation generally depends upon:

(a) whether it can be said that the corporation is vicariously liable for another; or

(b) where the person who committed the offence (with the requisite mens rea) can be properly described as part of the controlling mind of the corporate. It will generally be the position that corporates will not be guilty where the offence is punished by corporal means. For example, corporates will not be guilty of murder as no effective sentence could be levied: see *Hawke* v *Hutton* [1909] 2 KB 93 (cf manslaughter, *R* v *P&O European Ferries (Dover) Ltd* 92 Cr App R 72).

A controlling officer's actions will often bind the company personally (and not vicariously) as guilty of an offence. In *Tesco Supermarkets Ltd* v *Nattrass* [1972] A.C. 153 it was held that the person in such a situation is acting "as" the company since a company cannot actually think at all. Therefore he acts as the "embodiment" of the company and not simply as a servant thereof. If therefore he holds a guilty mind, so does the company. There must be one individual who, by his own thoughts and actions, is criminally responsible. It is not possible to aggregate differing thoughts and actions of various people within the company in order to come up with a composite guilty mind of the company.

BUSINESS NAMES ACT 1985

The Act regulates the names by which businesses can operate and stipulates certain requirements of the same. By section 4 of the Act there is a requirement to state in legible characters on virtually all business correspondence and paperwork an address for service in addition to either the partners' names, the individual's name or the corporate name (depending on the status of the business). There is also a requirement to display such names prominently to premises which the customers / suppliers have access.

Where there are 20 or more partners, compliance will be achieved by a clear reference to the fact that a list is maintained at the registered office and for which it is open to inspection.

In the course of business in this area is satisfied if it is done in part of the business activities.

With the increasing levels of e-communication it is essential that such requirements are borne in mind. Each employee who communicates in the course of business may well attract scrutiny under these sections, for which, of course, the employer may face responsibility. Section 7 illustrates the offences which exist by virtue of this Act.

The exact status of e-communications under this Act is not clear at present.

COMPANIES ACT 1985

The Act lays down similar requirements as the Business Names Act (above). By virtue of section 349 there is a requirement that all business letters, notices, other publications, bills of exchange, promissory notes, endorsements, cheques and orders for money or goods purported to be signed by or on behalf of the company and in all its bills of parcels, invoices, receipts and letters of credit, shall bear the legible name of the company. Failure to do so will result in a fine.

Any officer of a company who signs on behalf of the company a promissory note, bill of exchange, endorsement, cheque or order for money or goods in which the company's name is not mentioned as required is liable to a fine and personally liable to the holder of the item for the amount stated on it (unless it is duly paid by the company).

There is a similar requirement under section 351 to state in business letters (though the section is headed "Particulars in correspondence etc" – a wider definition arguably including e-communication) the company's place of registration and the registration number along with the address, and if applicable that it is a limited or an investment company. On stationery used for such letters or on the company's order forms any reference to share capital must be to the paid up share capital.

As stated above, it is essential that proper consideration is given to these matters, especially given the gradual expansion of e-mail as opposed to standard written documentation.

LIABILITY OF INTERNET SERVICE PROVIDERS: THE FUTURE

Elsewhere in this work (see chapter on defamation) the liability of ISPs has been considered. In this area is an important recent Directive: 2000/31/EC. By section 4, Articles 12 – 15 the Directive sets out certain obligations upon such providers.

By Article 12 the Directive identifies those service providers who are mere conduits. Those who fall within this definition are not liable for information transmitted on condition that the provider:

(a) does not initiate the transmission;

(b) does not select the receiver of the transmission ; and,

(c) does not select or modify the information contained in the transmission.

The transmission and provision of access include the automatic, intermediate and transient storage of the material transmitted, but only if this takes place for the "sole purpose of carrying out the transmission in the communication network, and provided that the information is not stored for any period longer than is reasonably necessary for the transmission" (Article 12, paragraph 2).

Similar provisions apply where the "sole purpose" is for making the onward transmission more efficient to those who request the information (see Article 13). This is subject to the provider:

(a) not modifying the information;

(b) complying with conditions on access to the information;

(c) complying with the industry standard for updating the information;

(d) not interfering with the lawful use of technology widely recognised and used by the industry to obtain data on the use of the information;

(e) acting expeditiously to remove, or disable access to, information which it has stored "upon obtaining actual knowledge of the fact that the information at the initial source of the transmission has been removed from the network, or access to it has been disabled, or that a court or an administrative authority has ordered such removal or disablement".

Similarly the Directive provides for non liability where a service provider unwittingly hosts information (see Article 14). There are similar provisions as to actual knowledge and as to removing any information expeditiously once identified.

By virtue of Article 15, the Directive states that there is no general obligation to monitor information which they transmit or store. Instead the Directive aims to encourage the industry and the State to regulate the ISPs by drawing up of codes of conduct: see Article 15. The Directive must be implemented by member states by 17 January 2002.

CHAPTER 15
DISCIPLINE OF EMPLOYEES

INTRODUCTION

Employers may well seek to regulate the use and abuse of the e-mail and internet facilities with which they provide their employees. Indeed, in certain circumstances, employers will be vicariously responsible for such abuses. As such it is small wonder that there is likely to be a proliferation of disciplinary action and dismissals related to e-mails. In doing the same the employers will enter the realm of employment law and must therefore balance on the legal tightrope very carefully given that the jurisprudence in this area is at its inception.

This chapter aims to identify the main areas of employment law that will be affected. The chapter gives guidance and analysis on dismissals, disciplinary action, discrimination and harassment and finally the use of e-mail policies.

DISCIPLINARY MATTERS

In order to discipline employees for internet misbehaviour or unauthorised use of e-mails, and the like, employers are advised to have set out, in writing if possible, the disciplinary procedure along with a non-exhaustive list of what will lead to disciplinary action.

Notifying employees as to what is and is not permitted is vital. Any discipline meted out without such notice could well lead to a claim for breach of contract (implied term of mutual trust and confidence), discrimination, harassment or constructive dismissal (see below).

Matters which will no doubt be the chief source of discipline will be the extraction of pornography (see Chapter 5) and the overuse of e-mail for personal messages. These should be expressly set out as forbidden in order to avoid the risk of having to justify disciplinary action. Each employer will have their own individual levels of tolerance. However, it is noted that as employees spend more and more time at work and the level of services increase to be internet based, it will be generally expected that a minimal use of e-mail would be acceptable. This would reflect the existing situation with personal calls from work.

The "punishment should fit the crime" and accordingly the extraction of obscene material on a regular basis may properly lead to dismissal whereas arranging a doctor's appointment is unlikely to justify any punishment. It is imperative that employers apply any discipline consistently and equally to all employees. Differences in treatment may otherwise imply favouritism, unfairness or even discrimination.

CONSTRUCTIVE DISMISSAL

An employee may be entitled to resign in reaction to his employer's behaviour and claim that he has been dismissed (see for instance section 95 Employment Rights Act 1996). In this context, if the discipline is such that the employee feels that his employer has breached their mutual contract then the employee may leave the company and claim constructive dismissal.

In order to succeed in his action, the evidence would have to show:

(a) that the level of conduct on the part of the employer entitled the employee to leave as he did, and

(b) that the employee did actually leave *because* of such treatment.

It has been propounded that the test for (a) is to effectively ask – did the employer breach the contract between them? (see *Western Excavating (ECC) Limited* v *Sharp* [1978] QB 761). The breach can, of course, be of the implied term of mutual trust and confidence between employer and the employed.

EXAMPLE

Surf chick Alex Issa is employed by graphic design giant Etienne Abrahams PLC which has a company policy stating "It shall be a disciplinary matter if any employee uses the e-mail system for personal uses". Alex Issa uses her work e-mail, contrary to the company policy, to arrange a surfing holiday. She works between 8.30am and 7pm five days a week and uses the e-mail 10 times for this purpose. She has been employed by Etienne Abrahams PLC for ten blemish-free years. Etienne Abrahams PLC call a disciplinary meeting, where Joe Kennealy, the managing director, suspends Alex Issa from work, and pay, for one month. Alex Issa says that she feels that she has no option but to leave and consequently resigns.

Alex Issa will be entitled to present a complaint to the Employment Tribunal within 3 months (see below) complaining that she has been constructively dismissed and seek compensation for unfair dismissal. The Tribunal will look at the circumstances and probably determine that the punishment was far too harsh and conclude that the decision to leave on Alex Issa's part was reasonable. Etienne Abrahams PLC would face paying compensation despite the fact that they did not dismiss Alex Issa.

UNFAIR DISMISSAL

Where the conduct is such that the employer feels it necessary to dismiss the employee concerned then the employee may well bring a claim for unfair dismissal. This is a statutory right now contained within the Employment Rights Act 1996 (section 94). The fairness or otherwise of a dismissal is dealt with by section 98.

It is for the employer to show that the reason for dismissal was:

1. related to capability or qualifications;

2. related to the conduct of the employee;

3. related to redundancy;

4. contravention of a statutory provision; or

5. for some other substantial reason;

AND that the dismissal was justifed, which depends upon whether, in the circumstances (including the size and administrative resources of the employer's undertaking) the employer acted reasonably in treating it as a sufficient reason for dismissing the employee and shall be determined in accordance with equity and the substantial merits of the case.

The test for unfair dismissal is therefore flexible and it will depend upon not only the conduct complained of, but also the size of the company and the overall circumstances of the case. The role of the tribunal is to consider whether the employer acted reasonably and not whether the tribunal would have acted in the same way. In doing so the tribunal must consider whether the employers acted within the band of reasonable responses open to them (see, for example *British Leyland UK Ltd* v *Swift* [1981] IRLR 91 (CA)).

In the present scenario the dismissals will predominantly relate to conduct. In *BHS Ltd* v *Burchell* [1980] ICR 303n, and subsequent cases, it has been held that in order for conduct dismissals to be seen as fair a three stage test should *generally* be applied:

(a) that the employer genuinely believed that the employee was guilty of misconduct;

(b) that belief must have been formed on reasonable grounds; and,

(c) the employer must have entered into a reasonable investigation.

(see also ACAS handbook, *Discipline at Work*).

In *Denco Limited* v *Joinson* [1991] IRLR 63 the employee had authorisation to enter certain menus on the computer system, but not others. Nevertheless he managed to obtain access to a menu for which he had no authorisation. The menu related to wages for other employees in a subsidiary company. The employer dismissed the employee without notice. The employee complained to a tribunal. The Employment Appeal Tribunal found in the following terms:

> "…if an employee deliberately uses an unauthorised password in order to enter or to attempt to enter a computer known to contain information to which he is not entitled, then that of itself is gross misconduct which prima facie will attract summary dismissal, although there may be some exceptional circumstances in which such a response might be held unreasonable…However, because of the importance of preserving the integrity of a computer with its information it is important that management should make it abundantly clear to its workforce that interfering with it will carry severe penalties"

The employer may also wish to rely upon the assertion that the dismissal was for "some other substantial reason". This is a "catch all" provision in section 98 and intended to allow the tribunal to keep flexibility in mind. The reasons often relate to economic scenarios (e.g. simply not being able to afford to keep the employee in question), but this is certainly not fixed. Employers may find this reason useful where the use (or misuse) of the internet cannot be said to amount to conduct justifying dismissal, but for some other substantial reason it constituted a good reason to dismiss. It is, however, highly unlikely that it will have any effect save in the most bizarre of cases and conduct is almost certainly to be the reason for dismissal in the large majority.

The fairness or otherwise of dismissal will depend upon all the circumstances of the case. There has already been a proliferation of dismissals relating to e-mail and internet use. In the case of *Lois Franxhi* v *Focus Management Consultants Limited* (see *Commercial Law Journal*, Jan/Feb 2000 page 23) the Applicant was fired for using the internet to surf for a holiday. The Applicant claimed that she was dismissed unfairly. The Tribunal found that the dismissal was reasonable on the grounds of misconduct (though this could partly have been based on previous misconduct). It was clear that the Tribunal were not convinced that simply failing to notify employees was enough, on its own, to render any dismissal unfair.

In *Humphries* v *VH Barnett & Co* (case number 2304001/97, July 1998, London (South) Employment Tribunal) it was held that mere unauthorised use would not "ordinarily" justify summary dismissal unless the company had expressly set out that it constituted gross misconduct.

The reasonableness or otherwise of a dismissal will always be considered taking all the circumstances into account. For instance, if an employee is dismissed for obtaining information by unauthorised use of the internet (or intranet), but the actual information could have been obtained by him legitimately by other means, then it is likely that dismissal would be viewed as too harsh a penalty (depending on the individual circumstances): see for example *British Telecommunications plc* v *Rodrigues* (EAT, 854/92, 20 February 1995).

In *Pennington and Beverley* v *Holset Engineering Limited* (unrep. Case numbers 1802184/00; 1802185/00, Leeds Employment Tribunal). The two Applicants claimed unfair dismissal when they were dismissed following their own private use of the e-mail system. The company concerned had made it clear that computers were to be used for work purposes only. There were clear warnings in relation to the consequences of internet misuse. The Applicants both sent offensive e-mails on more than one occasion. The company took action against those who had sent the material and not those who received it. The company treated the dismissal as for misuse of the electronic systems intended for business use. The Tribunal found the dismissal to be a potentially fair dismissal on the grounds of conduct. They then went on to consider the reasonableness of the decision. They went on to find that the misconduct was serious enough to warrant a dismissal and that there was a proper investigation.

The employers had drawn up an offensive rating list and ranked certain employees according to the level of offensiveness and the amount of e-mails which were sent. The Tribunal accepted that this had an element of subjectivity, but nevertheless was fair and reasonable. In the circumstances the Tribunal considered that the dismissals were within the band of reasonable responses of a reasonable employer.

In *Gale* v *Parknotts Limited* (case number 72487/95, 17 April 1996 Leeds Employment Tribunal) the employee concerned downloaded inoffensive material for his own use. This included a computer game. He was given a warning in relation to this. At a later date the computer system was crashed by a computer virus which was traced to the computer game downloaded before his warning. He was dismissed on the basis of a breach of trust. The Tribunal found the dismissal unfair, holding that it was not a breach of trust for an employee to put inoffensive material on the computer system before any warning was given. There was no evidence to trace the crash to any material downloaded *after* the warning.

It is suggested that there is also a slight distinction to be drawn between users who specifically connect to the internet for personal use and then disconnect when finished and those who work for companies who have permanent connections and therefore their personal use of the internet costs nothing save employer's time. In the former case the employer has paid for a call he otherwise would not have made and also lost his employee's time. This may be viewed as a more serious matter.

Employers should make it clear that the mere forwarding of e-mails will also be a matter leading to disciplinary procedures. The repetition of a defamation can still amount to defamation despite the material not being original (see chapter 6). Thus employees should be left in no doubt that forwarding e-mails, etc, is to be regarded in the same light as creating the same (see e-mail policies, below).

The fairness of dismissals will obviously also be linked to the kind of employment that one is concerned with. For instance, if highly confidential information is entrusted to a certain employee and that is inadvertently, but negligently, disclosed to third parties by e-mail, then it may warrant immediate dismissal. Whereas, if the information disclosed is not confidential in any way, the disclosure of it may not be such a serious matter. In *Winder* v *The Commissioners of the Inland Revenue* (case number 1101770/97, 20 April 1998 Ashford Employment Tribunal) the employee was employed as a valuation officer. The employee had communicated with a right wing organisation offering to disclose sensitive information. The employee was dismissed before such disclosure had taken place on the grounds of misconduct. The internal rules provided for the confidentiality of information. The dismissal was held to be fair on the basis that it was reasonable to conclude that the offer to obtain such information by using the computer system was a breach of the duty to maintain confidence.

Dismissals will also be linked to the kind of conduct alleged. Downloading pornography will be viewed more seriously than using the internet for merely e-mailing friends. This may be so even where the latter use is for a greater amount of time given the obscene nature of the same. It will be obvious to most employees that the use of the internet for pornographic purposes will not be permitted by their employers (even if it is not obvious that dismissal will necessarily result).

However, many employees see e-mail as a legitimate means of communication between friends at other companies, and would not necessarily think that it is not permitted by their employers (unless told to the contrary).

Where the employer alleges that the employee has misused the e-mail system it is suggested that a fair and proper investigation into the alleged misuse is carried out before the decision to dismiss is made. This will greatly assist when asserting that the dismissal was fair and reasonable. This is the subject of a recently reported decision of the EAT: *John Lewis plc* v *Coyne* (Times LR, 5 January 2001).

Use of e-mail in good business practice

Employers have a duty to consult with employees about a range of subjects (for instance variation of contracts, proposed redundancies, etc). Consultation has often taken the form of placing notices on boards, informing employee representatives, circulating documents or other methods. When consultation, or lack thereof, has become an issue at the tribunal it has often been a question of one word against another as to whether certain consultation was entered into with that particular employee (e.g. "I did not see the notice and no-one told me personally"). This is clearly undesirable.

The solution in the past has been to simply allocate more resources to the procedure. For instance, circulating a document which required a signature of confirmation which had to be collected by an employer representative. This was often time consuming and more costly. Now, however, there is a more economical way to avoid such issues. By the use of e-mail with a receipt function employers can ensure that all employees (even in vast undertakings) receive personal notification of any proposed changes. The system can ensure that employers have full information as to whether the notices have been read.

Intranet and e-mails offer, therefore, a great vehicle of information to employees. This can apply not only to obligations upon the employers, but also for internal employee groups to circulate information about the company and allow a good channel of communication between the same without, perhaps, the employer being required to allocate hours of working time for employee groups to meet.

It also means that employers can easily keep records of what has been said, read and understood. This may prove invaluable evidence in the instance of a dispute (see chapters 3 and 4 for related subjects).

Notification of e-mail offences

For an employer to avoid a claim for unfair dismissal it must be shown that the reason for the dismissal was legitimate (see above) and that the dismissal was fair and reasonable. This latter requirement involves an element of procedural fairness. Importantly, notice of the fact that personal use of the internet is misconduct and also the sanctions for the same.

EXAMPLE

JM Co. Ltd is a leading producer of computer components. Garry Wright is a senior computer programmer within the company working on the computer and the internet. He uses the internet on average for one hour per day for personal use. There is no company policy and the managing director also uses the internet for personal use for approximately 30 minutes per day. Garry Wright is dismissed for personal use of the internet. He is given no prior warning but is given his full contractual notice. Garry Wright claims unfair dismissal.

Garry Wright has clearly been using the internet for personal use and during his employer's time. However, in determining the fairness of the dismissal the Tribunal will consider that the lack of a policy, the lack of a warning, and the lack of any action taken against others may suggest the dismissal unfair in all the circumstances.

Now consider that JM Co. Ltd had expressly set out in an amended contract of employment (which had been agreed) that "any personal use of the internet will be considered gross misconduct and the employee may face immediate dismissal", and that Garry Wright had been personally warned of this in the past. The dismissal may be found to be fair and reasonable in such circumstances. It is of relevance, but by no means more than that, that the managing director has not been dismissed. The Tribunal's role is to establish whether Garry Wright has been fairly dismissed and not whether another employee may have, or should have, been dismissed as well. Evidentially, of course, the disparate treatment of employees may suggest unfairness or even unlawful discrimination.

Remedies

The tribunal can order:

(1) reinstatement (i.e. being placed back with his employers in the same role);

(2) re-engagement (i.e. being placed back with his employers in a different role); or,

(3) compensation only.

The former two may also include compensation. The award for compensation will include a basic award (worked out in a similar way as statutory redundancy) plus a compensatory award (i.e. the loss which flowed from the dismissal). There is a limit to compensation that currently stands at £50,000 in the large majority of cases.

Compensation can be reduced where the tribunal consider that there has been contributory fault by the employee. In *Dunn* v *IBM UK Ltd* (case number 2305087/97, 1 July 1998, London (South) Employment Tribunal) the Applicant was accessing pornography via the company's internet facility. The Applicant was dismissed. The Tribunal found such a dismissal too be too serious a reaction on the facts of the case and that it was therefore unfair. However, the Tribunal went on to consider that the Applicant had contributed to his own dismissal and therefore reduced his compensation by 50%.

Other Matters

The Tribunal should only entertain complaints of unfair dismissal which have been presented "before the end of the period of three months beginning with the effective date of termination, or within such further period as the tribunal considers reasonable in a case where it is satisfied that it was not reasonably practicable for the complaint to be presented before the end of that period of three months" (see section 111(2)).

Employees, full-time and part-time, attract the protection of unfair dismissal after working continuously for the employer for one year: see section 108 Employment Rights Act 1996, but not before.

BREACH OF CONTRACT

Irrespective of the possible claims for unfair dismissal, there is always the law of contract to govern relationships between employees and employers. Gross misconduct could amount to a repudiation of the contract and thereby sever such relationships without the need to give the usual contractual notice.

Where dismissals are in breach of contract and where proper notice is not given, employers may find themselves the subject of wrongful dismissal proceedings. Guarding against the same is no more onerous than for unfair dismissals and the reason that it is flagged up at this stage is twofold:

(1) there is no requirement for either minimum qualifying service or to present a claim within 3 months (instead the limitation for contract is 6 years), and

(2) compensation is not limited to £50,000.

As such when senior employees are dismissed, employers should not consider their liability limited.

Where claims are made for a breach of contract in the manner and procedure applied for disciplinary action, it is to be remembered that it is for the employer to decide on the disciplinary procedure to be followed in accordance with the terms of the contract and not in terms of reasonableness generally: see *Saeed* v *Royal Wolverhampton Hospitals NHS Trust* Times LR, 17 January 2001 (CA).

DISCRIMINATION AND HARASSMENT

Discrimination is unlawful by virtue of statutes in three main areas: sex, race and disability (Sex Discrimination Act 1975, Race Relations Act 1976, and the Disability Discrimination Act 1995). Discrimination is "less favourable treatment" on the grounds of, e.g., sex. The scope of discrimination is beyond this work, but it is essential, as pointed out elsewhere in this work, that employers treat all employees equally and on objective criteria. Harassment is a particular form of discrimination which amounts to acts or statements which can be said to harass an individual due to their, e.g. sex. The acts need not be persisting over time and one remark may, if serious enough, constitute harassment (see *Insitu Cleaning Co Ltd* v *Heads* [1995] IRLR 4). Less favourable treatment need still be shown.

Employers can be liable directly, for acts that they have committed, or vicariously for acts of their employees (see chapter 14). Direct liability will also be shown where it is found that the employer failed to adequately supervise the employees and thereby prevent harassment. In *Morse* v *Future Reality Limited* (case number 54571/95, 22 October 1996, London (North) Employment Tribunal) the Applicant shared an office with several male colleagues. The male colleagues downloaded pornographic and offensive material and referred a small amount on to the Applicant, the majority of the activity went on in the background. The activities were not directed at her personally, but made the Applicant feel uncomfortable. Following her resignation the Applicant complained of sexual harassment on the basis of the pornography and poor atmosphere. Detrimental impact was held to be established and the Applicant succeeded in her action. See also the recent case of *Waters* v *MPC* [2000] 1 WLR 1607.

It is easy to see that harassment claims of such a nature will be likely to increase. E-mail and internet combined will allow for the easier dissemination of offensive material and with it the transmission between employees of information which may seem to some humorous, but to others offensive.

It is also prudent to note that there is no limit to compensation for discrimination as there is with unfair dismissal.

Employers should, therefore, have clear policies on the use of the internet / e-mail system and should aim to supervise the same in the best way possible. The use of mail sweeping services so that offensive words are automatically omitted or so that there is some form of regulation will probably assist in removing direct responsibility from employers leaving only vicarious responsibility, the effects of which can be mitigated by surveillance (see Chapter 3) and ample punishment for the employees concerned.

E-MAIL POLICIES

This chapter has identified several reasons for having policies on the use of the internet, intranet and the use of e-mail. Each company will have its own threshold of regulation and hence will require differing contractual terms.

In deciding what terms should be drafted, the following may be of assistance (but are given by way of example only):

(1) Staff may not access the internet / external e-mail system for any purpose whatsoever without prior written permission from a member of managerial staff;

(2) No information which is unlawful, defamatory, lewd, obscene, or otherwise inappropriate, or likely to result in any form of liability on the part of the company, is to be stored, sent, forwarded, downloaded, printed, or otherwise dealt with, whilst using the company's systems. All information transmitted by the company must reflect the standards, business practice and policies of the company;

(3) Internet, intranet and e-mail facilities are intended for business use only and are not considered private. The company reserves the right to carry out reasonable and proportionate surveillance of e-mail and the internet, including deleted items, and employees are put on notice that the same will commence without further notice. Notice of the type, extent and means of surveillance will be displayed on the employee notice board and copies will be available from the personnel department;

(4) All confidential communications by e-mail must be encrypted, regardless of the nature and destination of the information;

(5) Employees' computer passwords are confidential to that employee alone. No such password should be disclosed to any others for whatever purpose without the prior written permission from a member of managerial staff;

(6) Any external transmissions should have the appropriate legal requirements, including confidentiality notices, disclaimers and signature
files;

(7) Employees should treat communications by e-mail as they would a
letter. The style and content of an e-mail should be written accordingly;

(8) Where employees are permitted to use the internet and / or e-mail and
/ or intranet system they must adhere to the law in all respects including, but not limited to, refraining from making any critical or defamatory statements about other individuals or companies (howsoever
intended), respecting copyright, refraining from making or forwarding
any material or information which has the potential to be offensive to
others on the grounds of gender, race, disability or religious grounds,
or any other such information which is not written in accordance with
the business practices, policies and standards of the company.

The use of terms and conditions and / or company handbooks is a good way
of both notifying the employees of the rules and preventing any infringement
of the same and the consequent liability to third parties. It should be made
clear that policies represent business practice and that all employees must
adhere to the policy. The changes should be notified to each employee when
they occur. The failure to adhere to the policy should be referred to as potential gross misconduct with the possible sanction of summary dismissal.

Employers are recommended to have the internet / e-mail policy well publi-
cised and acknowledged by employees and any representative body. The
acceptance of the terms and conditions should also be sought. It is also very
important to have a policy which is both realistic and proportionate. A company which openly permits personal e-mails, but has a policy of full restriction, may be at risk of finding that they are prevented from relying upon the
policy due to the acquiescence which they have shown over a period of time.
It is suggested therefore that careful drafting is in order to tailor the policy to
the exact company's requirements. In this vein the examples above are for
illustration only and legal advice should be sought in drafting any policy.

For a precedent e-mail policy, see Duggan *Contracts of Employment*, 2001.

For an informative analysis of e-mail policies see IDS Study 682, *Internet and e-
mail policies* (January 2000).

CHAPTER 16

INSURANCE

INTRODUCTION

This Chapter sets out some of the implications of the increase in liabilities caused by the use of e-mail on both insured and insurers.

INCREASED RISKS

The use of the internet has created ever greater risks for those selling goods and services as well as for employers and employees. Not only are there the inter-jurisdictional risks such as the possibility of being caught by consumer protection legislation in each country but also there are the expanded number of offences and torts which may be committed in the virtual world. In addition, there is the risk of technical failure through for example, viruses.

The natural way of dealing with these increased risks is to look to insurance. However, this comes at a cost and only time will tell how insurance companies will deal with this. Clearly there is an opportunity to open up new market for the insurance industry. The alternative is that the industry effectively buries its head in the sand and simply puts in disclaimers with regard to remote potential offences, torts and other liabilities which may arise.

An example of a recent case which highlights the need for insurance in the context of the duty of care held by computer consultants in *Stephenson Blake (Holdings) Ltd* v *Streets Heaver Limited* (noted by Sarah Ahmed in *Computers and Law* August/September 1999, pages 38–40).

PURCHASERS OF INSURANCE

Full disclosure

Those buying insurance contracts should be careful to fully disclose all of their internet and e-mail activity and even their use of mobile phones. In the absence of this, there is always the risk that insurance companies may refuse to indemnify on the basis of material non-disclosure.

The duty of full disclosure and good faith was emphasised in the case of *CTI International Inc. & Anor* v *Oceanus Mutual Underwriting Association (Bermuda) Ltd (1984)* FTCR 10.2.84. The case concerned an appeal by underwriters against the rejection of a defence under s.18 Marine Insurance Act 1906 in a claim by a container leasing company. The Court of Appeal held that the history of the case was riddled by material non-disclosures by a director of a firm of Lloyd's brokers acting for the Claimant. The defendants had been kept in ignorance of the fact that Lloyd's had stopped paying claims until completion of investigations they were making. The presentation of the risk had fallen short of the requirement of utmost good faith called for by the Act and therefore the appeal was allowed.

Policy exclusions

Purchasers of insurance should also be careful to check the terms of any insurance that they take out in order to check that any of their potential liabilities are not excluded.

Scope of insurance policies

Firms should also consider whether to extend the scope of their present insurance. For example, given the current uncertainties in the area of internet and e-mail law, there is much scope for expensive and controversial test cases as the principles are bashed out in the courts. With this in mind, purchasers should be careful to take out legal expenses policies and potentially ones which will cover such an eventuality.

It is interesting to note that the solicitors' professional insurance is switching from the Solicitors Indemnity Fund to the open market. During this process, solicitors should be particularly careful to check their cover given their increased risks by any internet and e-mail activity, in particular the possibility of professional negligence actions based upon on-line advice. See in this regard the Solicitors' Indemnity Insurance Rules 2000.

INSURERS

Insurers on the other hand need to be careful to factor in the increased risks presented by the new economy. It may be at present that their policies cover such risks. In such circumstances, they will be bound to indemnify even though they have failed to take account of such risk in the premium.

Insurers also need to be clear about the duty of disclosure and it would be helpful if they were to make this explicit in their guidance and contracts.

Clearly, there is an enormous commercial opportunity to be exploited. Even if mainstream insurers followed a course of simply adding disclaimers to their present contracts, it seems highly unlikely that any such gap in the market would remain for very long. As part of that exploitation, it will be in insurers' interests to raise public awareness as to the potential risks of having a presence on-line. This can only be helpful to all.

PART 4: ON-LINE CONTRACTS

CHAPTER 17
FORMATION OF A CONTRACT

"The Internet is like a gold-rush; the only people making money are those who sell the pans."

Will Hobbs, IUMA

INTRODUCTION

One of the major effects of the internet revolution is the ability to buy and sell on-line. About a year ago, figures suggested that the worldwide revenue generated from the web by American companies was $301.4 billion which would make it the world's thirteenth largest economy. In 2000, the internet was predicted to become more important to the US economy than cars, energy or telecommunications and the internet economy probably to become bigger than Spain's (ninth largest in the world). [Sources: OECD/IMF/University of Texas].

As consumers have moved from high street shopping (ironically called "s-commerce" in one anonymous e-mail which did the rounds) to the internet, numerous legal questions have been raised, many of which have not yet been resolved. Invitations to treat, offers and acceptance have to be translated into the electronic world. So, too, the choice of law and within that what rights the consumer may have.

This book is intended to provide a brief introduction to all of these issues although for a fuller exposition in-depth text-books on contract law, conflict of laws and consumer law would need to be consulted.

A major development in the law of on-line contracting is the Electronic Communications Act 2000 which is dealt with in Chapter 4, above.

This Chapter provides an introduction to the law on the formation of a contract and highlights the difficulties that the application of traditional legal concepts to the making of contracts by e-mail may present.

INVITATION TO TREAT, OFFER AND ACCEPTANCE

Shop

A price tag on a good sitting in a shop is treated under English law as an invitation to treat. This means that it does not constitute an offer by the shop which the consumer could accept and thereby bind the shop. The consumer must approach the cash desk then make an offer which the shop is at liberty to accept or reject.

Internet sites

The same analysis probably applies with respect to internet sites which offer goods and services on-line. However, this remains to be seen and to avoid any doubt any companies with such a site would be well-advised to make it clear that all prices and descriptions are invitations to treat.

The next difficulty arises when a customer fills in a form on-line then enters it on the web-site. Many sites give access to their standard terms and conditions and enter a term on the main page providing that the customer has read and accepts the terms and conditions. At end of the transaction, very often there is a section providing that the transaction is completed. This would suggest that potentially the site is explicitly making an offer which the customer is at liberty to accept there and then. Other sites stipulate that the transaction is subject to confirmation by the seller. This would be the advisable practice for those wishing to avoid any such doubt.

E-mail

The same analysis would apply where a web-site advertises goods or services and provides that they may be ordered by e-mail, giving the e-mail address and perhaps a link to Outlook Express to facilitate that process.

A different situation arises again when a customer receives an e-mail from a company advertising goods or services. It is likely that these would get treated like terrestrial advertising whereby the details merely constitute an invitation to treat.

Ambiguity arises due to the fact that any such e-mails are specifically addressed to an individual even though they may have been part of a block e-mail. In these circumstances, it may be argued that such an e-mail constitutes a specific and personalised offer.

Once again, this matter remains to be decided and the best course would appear to be for companies to make the status of such dealings clear in their initial communication.

WAP/SMS

Such analysis would also apply to purchases made by WAP and SMS.

PLACE OF CONCLUSION OF CONTRACT

Postal rule

It should be remembered that whilst offers and withdrawals of offers need to actually be communicated to the other party, the rules governing acceptance are different. Where acceptance is made by a means which is instantaneous such as face to face or orally, the rule is that acceptance must reach the other side.

However, where an acceptance is made in written form, in English law the so-called 'postal-rule' applies. This provides that the acceptance is deemed to have been made at the time that the letter is posted, not when it arrives or indeed whether it arrives or not (*Adams* v *Lindsell* (1818) 1 B & Ald 681).

The question therefore arises as to whether or not the postal rule applies to electronic communications. In this context, it has been held that telex communications are instantaneous and therefore the postal rule does not apply to contracts made by telex and acceptance is made when it is received (*Entores Ltd* v *Miles Far Eastern Corporation* [1955] 2 QB 327). It is likely that such an approach will be taken to e-mails and other forms of communications where there is a direct link between the parties. Obviously, this is subject to the assumption that the law governing the contract (dealt with in the next chapter) has a postal or equivalent rule.

A more difficult situation arises where an electronic communication is sent across a network which stores the message for some time before it is delivered to the other party. In this situation, it is quite possible that the postal rule might apply. The dictum of Lord Brandon in *Brinkibon Ltd* v *Stahag Stahl und Stahlwarenhandelgesellschaft mbH* [1982] 1 All ER 293, at page 300 supports such a conclusion:

> "The cases on acceptance by letter and telegram constitute an exception to the general principle of the law of contract [on grounds of expediency] ... That reason of commercial expediency applies to cases where there is bound to be a substantial interval between the time when the acceptance is sent and the time when it is received. In such cases the exception to the general rule is more convenient, and makes on the whole for greater fairness, than the rule itself would do."

It may also be argued that the postal rule should apply all the more so if the offer has been sent in the same form. This is because it could be said that the offeror has impliedly accepted the risk of using that form of communication by making the offer in the same manner.

A final complication in this respect is that even if the postal rules applies, the exact timing of the posting may be in doubt. It could be when the offeree presses *send* on his computer or alternatively when the network receives the communication. If the analogy with the snail mail is kept then it would seem more likely that it is when the network actually receives it. This would be the equivalent of the letter dropping into the post box.

However, it may be argued that the sending of the e-mail is like the dropping in the post box and that transmission to the network is merely like taking a letter to the sorting office. Only time will tell how the courts will deal with this problem.

Analogous situations

Instantaneous communications: the Citibank fraud case

The Citibank fraud case of *R* v *Governor of Brixton Prison and another, Ex parte Levin* [1996] 4 All ER 350 faced a similar issue. Citibank suffered a significant breach of security in its cash management system, resulting in funds being transferred from customer accounts into the accounts of the perpetrator and his accomplices. Eventually, Vladimir Levin was arrested in the United Kingdom and was eventually extradited to the United States. One of the issues in the extradition hearings revolved around the question of where the offences were held to have taken place. It was argued for the defendant that it occurred in St. Petersburg when Mr Levin pressed particular keys on the keyboard instigating fraudulent Citibank transfers. It was argued for the extradition applicant that the offence took place where the changes to the data occurred, the Citibank computer in Parsipenny in the United States. The judge decided in favour of the applicant on the basis that the real-time nature of the communication link between Levin and the Citibank computer meant that Levin's keystrokes were actually occurring on the Citibank computer.

In this context, it is also worth noting the cases on jurisdiction and tort set out in Chapter 18 below and in particular *Domicrest Ltd* v *Swiss Bank Corpn* [1999] QB 548 in which it was held that the place where the negligent misstatement giving rise to the damage occurs is where it originates, rather than where it is received and relied upon. In other words, with regards to a telephone conversation this is where the words are spoken rather than where they are heard.

Message-based systems such as e-mail

A message-based system of communication such a e-mail may have produced a different result. In *Governor of Pentonville Prison, Ex parte Osman* [1989] 3 All ER 701, the court held that the sending of a telex constituted the act of appropriation and, therefore, the place from where the telex was sent was where the offence was committed. It should be noted that this would produce a different result to that in *Brinkibon Ltd* v *Stahag Stahl und Stahlwarenhandelgesellschaft mbH* (above). The easiest explanation for this is that acceptance in contract simply applies a different test to that for the place of an offence. Alternatively, this inconsistency in approach may simply reflect the present confusion which exists in this area of law.

Web-page

In *R* v *Graham Lester Ian Waddon* [2000] LTL 6/4, the case concerned 11 offences of publishing obscene material, namely computer images on the internet, and one offence of publishing obscene material for public gain. It was submitted that the English Court had no jurisdiction since there had only been publication of a web-site in America and not in England. On this issue, the Court of Appeal noted that section 1(3)(b) Obscene Publications Act 1959 stated that publishing an article included data stored and transmitted electronically. In the face of that provision, counsel correctly, conceding as he did that W himself or through his agents was involved in both the transmission of material to a web-site and the sending back of the information to England, could not contend that publication of information did not take place in this country. The Court of Appeal was of the opinion that publication could take place when uploaded onto a web-site abroad and then again when downloaded elsewhere. What would appear on a computer screen would be regarded as on a par with a statement in a document.

Conclusion

The position still remains unclear at English law. It is to be hoped that with the implementation of the European E-Commerce Directive (see Chapter 20, below) that the Government will make it clear.

In any event, the English courts have accepted that it is permissible for the parties to stipulate what acts will constitute acceptance (see *Holwell Securities Ltd* v *Hughes* [1974] 1 WLR 155). For the moment it is therefore advisable that the parties stipulate exactly which law is to apply and when acceptance will take place.

For further analysis of the problem see *Computer Law*, 4th edition, 2000, edited by Chris Reed and John Angel.

EXAMPLE

On 1 June, leading Barrister Perrin Gibbons sends an e-mail to Mark Atwood Ballet Services Ltd ordering a ticket for a performance of Swan Lake on 2 August at 8pm. Mark Atwood replies by e-mail at 3pm on 2 June. In the meantime, Perrin Gibbons has changed her mind and cancels her order by e-mail. This is received by Mark Atwood at 3.01pm. Mark Atwood's acceptance is received by the network at 3.02pm and by Perrin Gibbons at 3.10pm.

If the postal rule applies and the time taken is the time Mark Atwood sent the reply, Perrin Gibbons will be bound by the original contract. If the time is when the network received the e-mail or alternatively if the postal rule is deemed not to apply, Perrin Gibbons will not be so bound.

CHAPTER 18
CONFLICT OF LAWS

One of the greatest legal difficulties presented by e-commerce arises from one of the great advantages of the internet: that it crosses national and jurisdictional boundaries. This immediately raises questions relating to the area of law described by lawyers as private international law or alternatively conflict of laws.

In particular, the two immediate questions in this context are:

(a) which law will apply to any contract or tort;

(b) would the English courts have jurisdiction to entertain an action based upon such a contract or tort.

This chapter provides only a brief guide to this subject and for more detailed expositions of the subject, readers are referred to the following texts which the authors have found particularly helpful: *The Conflict of Laws* by J.G. Collier (Second Edition, 1994), *Cheshire and North's Private International Law* by Sir Peter North and J.J. Fawcett (Thirteenth Edition, 1999), *The Conflict of Laws* by J.H.C. Morris (Fifth Edition, 2000) and *Clerk & Lindsell on Torts* (Seventeenth Edition, 1995).

CHOICE OF LAW

Contract

The choice of law which governs a particular contract is regulated by the Rome Convention 1980 which was enacted into English law with the Contracts (Applicable Law) Act 1990. It sets out rules which the courts must follow in order to determine what it describes as the 'applicable law' of the contract. For the purposes of this book, the following briefly sets out the main rules with regard to choice of law. It should be noted that separate rules cover the existence and material validity of a contract although these are less likely to be applicable to disputes involving e-mail than those set out below.

Express or inferred choice of law

The basic rules for the ascertainment of the applicable law are contained in Articles 3(1) and 4(1) of the Convention which provide that a contract 'shall be governed by the law chosen by the parties. Their choice must be express or demonstrated with reasonable certainty by the terms of the contract or the circumstances of the case' failing which, 'the contract shall be governed by the law of the country with which it is most closely connected.'

Imputed applicable law

Article 4(1) provides that in the absence of choice, the applicable law is to be 'the law of the country with which the contract is most closely connected'. In determining this law, Article 4 gives three presumptions.

The main one is article 4(2) which provides that the contract is presumed to be most closely connected with the country 'in which the party who is to effect the performance which is characteristic of the contract has, at the time of the conclusion of the contract his habitual residence'.

The other two presumptions relate to specific situations. Article 4(3) provides that contracts involving immovable property are presumed to be most closely connected with the country where the immovable property is situated. In the context of carriage of goods, Article 4(4) refers to the principal place of business of the carrier at the time that the contract was concluded.

Mandatory rules and public policy

Article 3(3) limits the application of the chosen law by providing that it 'shall not, where all the other elements relevant to the situation at the time of the choice are connected with one country only, prejudice the application of rules of the law of that country which cannot be derogated from by contract.'

This means that certain rules, generally governed by public policy, which apply in a particular law which is closely associated with the contract shall continue to apply whatever law the parties may have chosen.

An English example of such a law is the Unfair Contract Terms Act 1977 which is dealt with in the next chapter. Section 27(2) of the Act provides that the provisions of the Act have effect notwithstanding any contract term which applies or purports to apply the law of some country outside the United Kingdom where either or both of the following apply:

(a) in making the contract one of the parties dealt as a consumer when he was habitually resident in the United Kingdom and the essential steps in the making of the contract were taken in this country, in which case the provisions of the Act prevail;

(b) if the court or arbitrator concludes that the term was imposed wholly or mainly for the purpose of enabling the party who imposed it to evade the operation of the Act.

Thus, where a party is not a consumer the expressly chosen law will apply unless it was incorporated as an evasion device.

The effect of Article 3(3) is that it effectively includes the relevant mandatory rules within the contract itself.

Public policy

It should be noted that as a matter of public policy English courts will refuse to apply certain laws of other countries. This is allowed by Article 16 of the Convention.

Unlike the application of mandatory rules which effectively include certain extra provisions into a contract, the mechanism here is to exclude certain of the foreign laws which offend English public policy.

An example of this is a contract which will imperil the relations of the Crown with a foreign friendly power. To enforce such a contract would be regarded as contrary to the principle of international comity. In practice this means not enforcing a contract which would result in a criminal offence being committed in that other country.

An example is provided by the case of *Foster* v *Driscoll* [1929] 1 KB 470 in which a contract for the supply and sale of whiskey which it was intended should be smuggled into the United States and ultimately sold and consumed there in violation of the prohibition laws of the time was not enforced.

Consumer contracts

Article 5 provides a separate regime for consumer contracts. These are defined in Article 5(1) as contracts whose object "is the supply of goods or services to a person ("the consumer") for a purpose which can be regarded as outside his trade or profession, or a contract for the provision of credit for that object".

Article 5(2) provides that:

"Notwithstanding the provisions of Article 3, a choice of law made by the parties shall not have the result of depriving the consumer of the protection afforded to him by the mandatory rules of the law of the country in which he has his habitual residence:

– if in that country the conclusion of the contract was preceded by a specific invitation addressed to him or by advertising, and he had taken in that country all the steps necessary on his part for the conclusion of the contract, or

–   if the other party or his agent received the consumer's order in that country, or

–   if the contract is for the sale of goods and the consumer travelled from that country to another country and there gave his order, provided that the consumer's journey was arranged by the seller for the purpose of inducing the consumer to buy."

Article 5(3) provides that:

"Notwithstanding the provisions of Article 4, a contract to which this Article applies shall, in the absence of choice in accordance with Article 3, be governed by the law of the country in which the consumer has his habitual residence if it is entered into in circumstances described in paragraph 2 of this Article."

What these provisions effectively mean is that in general, a consumer will be protected by the mandatory laws of the country in which he has his habitual residence. Further, that in the absence of express or inferred choice, the law of his habitual residence will apply.

EXAMPLE

Movie mogul Mark 'Cricket Pads' Evans orders a bottle of wine from Roger Morris Enterprises based in Martigny, Switzerland. He orders it by e-mail from his penthouse flat overlooking Lords in London to be delivered to the same address. Roger Morris Enterprises' contract stipulates that the contract shall be governed by the law of the little known country of Porlock under which there are no rules on consumer protection. The contract also stipulates that the supplier will not be liable for any defects in the product or any harm which may result from its consumption. Mark Evans is poisoned by the wine, is unable to work for five weeks and loses a major film contract.

Mark Evans was acting as a consumer. Is he protected by the Unfair Contract Terms Act 1977?

Employment contracts

Article 6 of the Convention provides similar provisions for employment contracts. Article 6(2) provides that:

"Notwithstanding the provisions of Article 4, a contract of employment shall, in the absence of choice in accordance with Article 3, be governed:

(a) by the law of the country in which the employee habitually carries

out his work in performance of the contract, even if he is tem-
porarily employed in another country; or

(b) if the employee does not habitually carry out his work in any one
country, by the law of the country in which the place of business
through which he was engaged is situated;

unless it appears from the circumstances as a whole that the contract
is more closely connected with another country, in which case the
contract shall be governed by the law of that country."

What this effectively means is that in general, in the absence of choice, the
applicable law shall be that where the employee habitually carries out his work.

In addition to this, Article 6(1) provides that notwithstanding Article 3

"in a contract of employment a choice of law made by the parties
shall not have the result of depriving the employee of the protection
afforded to him by the mandatory rules of law which would be applicable under paragraph 2 in the absence of choice".

Therefore, in general, the employee shall be protected by the mandatory laws
of the country in which he habitually carries out his work.

Tort

Whilst this is less relevant to the law relating to e-mail, it is worth noting the
general principles for the few cases where torts may be committed through
the use of an e-mail.

Common law rules

The traditional English choice of law rules in tort derive from the case of *Phillips
v Eyre* [1870] LR 6 QB 1. Since the Private International Law (Miscellaneous
Provisions) Act 1995, these now only apply to defamation.

Broadly, it can be said that if the conduct occurs in England alone, English law
applies. Where the conduct takes place abroad, liability is determined by English
law, subject to the condition that, if liability exists by English law, it must also be
civilly actionable in damages by the law of the place where it took place.

There is some degree of flexibility in this rule and further complications arise
where both contractual and tortuous issues arise. However, for the purposes of
this book, it is the general rule which is worth remembering.

Private International Law (Miscellaneous Provisions) Act 1995 ("PILA 95")

This now applies to all torts other than defamation. The general rule is that
the applicable law is that of the country in which the events constituting the

tort in question occurred. But where elements of those events occur in different countries, the applicable law under the general rule is as follows:

(a) for a cause of action for personal injury or death resulting from personal injury, the law of the country where the individual was when he sustained the injury;

(b) for a cause of action in respect of damage to property, the law of the country where the property was when it was damaged; and

(c) in any other case, the law of the country in which the most significant elements of the events constituting the tort occurred.

However, if it appears, in all the circumstances, from a comparison of:

(a) the significance of the factors which connect a tort with the country whose law is the applicable law under the general rule; and

(b) the significance of factors connecting the tort with another country,

that it is substantially more appropriate for the applicable law for the determination of issues arising in the case, or any of the issues, to be the law of the other country, the general rule is displaced. The applicable law for determining those issues, as the case may be, is the law of that other country. The factors which may be taken into account as connecting a tort with a country for this purpose include, in particular, factors relating to the parties, to any events which constitute the tort in question or to any of the circumstances or consequences of those events.

It should be noted that in this context the Act does not authorise a court to apply another law where to do so would either conflict with the rules of public policy, or give effect to a penal, revenue or other public law which would not otherwise be enforceable here. Further, any rule of law which applies notwithstanding the rules of private international law is not prejudiced by this part of the Act.

JURISDICTION OF ENGLISH COURTS

The other main conflict of law issue in this area is whether the English courts have jurisdiction to entertain an action which has some foreign element.

European Union and EFTA

If the Defendant in a civil or commercial matter is domiciled in the European Union or a country which is a member of the European Free Trade Association ("EFTA") ("contracting states"), the Civil Jurisdiction and Judgments Acts

1982 and 1991 will apply which implemented the Brussels Convention 1968 on Jurisdiction and the Enforcement of Judgments in Civil and Commercial Matters and the Lugano Convention 1989.

General rule

The basic principle and the general rule governing jurisdiction is that persons domiciled in a contracting state, whatever their nationality, must be sued in the courts of that state alone (Article 2 of the Brussels Convention). This is subject to two exceptions:

(a) a defendant cannot be sued in the courts of his domicile if some other court has exclusive jurisdiction (article 16). The best example of this is where the issue concerns immovable property (i.e. land). The courts where the land is situated will then have exclusive jurisdiction.

(b) where the defendant is a party to a contractual agreement to submit to another jurisdiction (Article 17).

Domicile

An individual is domiciled in the United Kingdom or a particular part of it if he is both resident in and has a substantial connection with it. If he has no such substantial connection, his domicil is that part where he is resident. An individual is domiciled in a non-contracting state only if he is resident there and has a substantial connection with it.

A corporation is domiciled where it has its seat. This is in the United Kingdom if either:

(a) it was incorporated or formed under the law of a part thereof and has its registered office or some other official address therein; or

(b) its central management or control is exercised in the United Kingdom.

Contract

The Acts also provide that in addition to the general jurisdiction provided, there are certain situations where another country may also have jurisdiction subject again to Articles 16 and 17 mentioned above. These include contract, tort and insurance and consumer contracts.

With regard to matters relating to a contract, article 5(1) provides that the defendant may also be sued in the courts for the place of performance of the obligation in question.

In *Tessili* v *Dunlop* Case 12/76 [1976] ECR 1473; [1977] 1 CMLR 26, the European Court of Justice held that the national court before whom the action is brought must determine in accordance with its own rules on conflict of laws what is the law applicable to the legal relationship in question and define in accordance with that law the place of performance of the contractual obligation in question.

Tort

With regard to tort, article 5(3) provides that the defendant may also be sued in the courts where the harmful event occurred.

No Guidance is given in the Convention as to where this may be. In *Bier BV* v *Mines de Potasse D'Alsace SA* Case 21/76 [1978] QB 708; [1976] ECR 1735, it was alleged that the French defendants had polluted the waters of the Rhine in France. These waters flowed into the Netherlands where damage was caused to a Dutch horticultural business. The European Court of Justice held that article 5(3) was intended to cover both the place where the damage occurred and also the place of the event giving rise to it, where the two were not identical.

The *Bier* rule was applied by the Court of Justice in *Shevill* v *Presse Alliance SA* [1995] 2 AC 18 in which an English Claimant claimed for defamation based upon an article which appeared in *France Soir*, published by a French incorporated company. It was held that the claimant could sue either in the place where the damage occurred or the place which gave rise to and was at the origin of that damage.

The same principles as in the *Shevill* case have been applied in the analogous situation of copyright infringement involving publications in several Contracting States (see *Wegmann* v *Elsevier Science Ltd* [1999] I L Pr 379, French Cour de Cassation).

The analogy of defamation has also been applied in a case of negligent misstatement. In *Domicrest Ltd* v *Swiss Bank Corpn* [1999] QB 548, Rix J held that in such a case the place where the harmful event giving rise to the damage occurs is where the missstament originates, rather than where it is received and relied upon. In the case of a telephone conversation between persons in different countries, this is where the words constituting the misstatement are spoken (in the instant case, this was in Switzerland), rather than where they were heard (in the instant case, this was in England). Accordingly, the English court had no jurisdiction. There is no difference for these purposes between oral or other instantaneous communication and a written document.

Rix J refused to follow the earlier negligent misstatement case of *Minster Investments Ltd* v *Hyundi Precision and Industry Co. Ltd* [1988] 2 Lloyds Rep 621.

In this case, which was decided before *Shevill*, Steyn J decided to use a traditional English formula, and ask "where in substance the cause of action in tort arises, or what place the tort is most closely connected with". The essence of the action for negligent misstatement was said to be the negligent advice and reliance on it. Certificates negligently produced in France and Korea were received and relied upon in England. However, as Rix J pointed out, the 'substance' test does not reflect either the wording or the philosophy of the Convention as laid down in the European Court's decisions.

In any event, the claimant always has the option of suing in the place where the damage occurred, which is quite likely to be the place of receipt or reliance.

Clearly, the significance of this for e-mail and other electronic forms of communication is such that it suggests that instantaneous communications will be treated as arising in the place where the keyboard was pressed sending the message or document. E-mail may well be treated in the same way although this would seem to be a more controversial area.

Employment

Article 5(1) also applies to employment contracts. The place of performance of the obligation in question is defined as the place where the employee habitually carries out his work. Further, if the employee does not carry out his work in any one country, the employer may also be sued in the courts for the place where the business which engaged the employee was or is now situated.

Consumer contracts

Special rules were provided for certain consumer contracts in order to afford extra protection to consumers. Briefly, they are as follows.

A consumer may sue the supplier where either is domiciled. Where the supplier is not domiciled in a contracting state but has a branch, agency or other establishment in a contracting state, he is deemed to be domiciled there.

However, a consumer may generally only be sued where he is domiciled.

He may also be sued elsewhere by agreement. But the normal rules conferring jurisdiction by agreement do not apply. An agreement only confers jurisdiction over a consumer if:

(a) it was concluded after the dispute arose; or

(b) it allows the consumer to bring proceedings in a place other than those already indicated or in a member state in which both he and the supplier were domiciled or habitually resident when the contract was concluded.

Rest of the world

If the Defendant is not domiciled in a contracting state, then the English common law rules will govern jurisdiction. There are number of rules in this context.

- Presence

English Courts will have jurisdiction if the defendant is present in England when he is served with the writ or equivalent document.

For companies, it should be noted that in general, at common law a company will be deemed to be within the jurisdiction if it carries on business here;

- Submission

Submission also brings jurisdiction to the English courts. This may happen in one of four ways:

1. the defendant accepts service of the proves;

2. the defendant pleads to the merits of the case;

3. the defendant contracts to submit;

4. the claimant who is abroad sues a defendant here.

- Extended jurisdiction by service abroad

Order 11 rule 1(1) of the Rules of the Supreme Court gives authority to the court to assume jurisdiction over absent defendants in certain specified situations at the discretion of the court. The main provisions are:

(a) where the Defendant is domiciled within the jurisdiction;

(b) where an injunction is sought ordering the defendant to refrain from doing something within the jurisdiction;

(c) where the defendant is a necessary and proper party to proceedings;

(d) where there the claim involves a contract which:
    i.   was made within the jurisdiction;
    ii. was made by or through an agent trading or residing in the jurisdiction;
    iii. is by its terms or implication to be governed by English law;
    iv. contains a term to the effect that the High Court shall have jurisdiction;

  v. has been breached and where the breach was committed within
      the jurisdiction. It should be noted in this regard that English law
      determines where the breach was committed.
  e. Where the claim is founded on a tort and the damage was sustained,
      or resulted from and act committed, within the jurisdiction.

On-line complications

The law with regard to e-mail and the internet in this context clearly still
needs to be developed. A recent case which highlights some of the potential
problems is *Euromarket Designs Inc* v *Peters* (noted by Dawn Osborne in
Computers and Law, August/September 2000, pages 26–27).

The defendants ran a shop in Southern Ireland called Crate and Barrel and
also had a web-site. The claimant was an American business called Crate and
Barrel which had a UK trade-mark in that name. One of the issues in an application for summary judgment for infringement of the trademark was
whether the High Court of England had jurisdiction and one of the issues in
this regard was whether a reasonable trader would regard the use of the web-
site as "in the course of trade in relation to the goods" within the United
Kingdom.

Jacob J held that the web-site did not come within this test and would not
therefore give the court jurisdiction. The judge found it significant that the
site had an ".ie" (for Eire) domain name and further that it was clear that the
site related to a shop in Ireland. Nor was there any evidence that anyone in
the UK had regarded the site as directed at him. He continued:

> "Whether one gets there by a search or by direct use of the address, is
> it rational to say that the defendants are using the words "Crate and
> Barrel" in the UK in the course of trade in goods? If it is it must follow
> that the defendants are using it in every country of the world ... In
> 0800 Flowers [another case in which Jacob J gave judgment] I rejected
> the suggestion that the Web site owner should be regarded as putting
> a tentacle onto the user's screen. Mr Miller here used another analogy.
> He said using the Internet was like the user focusing a super telescope
> into the site concerned; he asked me to imagine such a telescope set
> up on the Welsh hills overlooking the Irish Sea. I think Mr Miller's
> analogy is very apt in this case. Via the web you can look into the
> defendant's shop in Dublin, indeed the very language of the internet
> conveys the idea of the user going to the site – "visit" is the word.
> Other cases would be different – a well known example, for instance,
> is amazon.com. Based in the US it has actively gone out to seek world-
> wide trade, not just by the name of the Internet but by advertising its
> business here, and offering and operating a real service of supply of
> books to this country. These defendants have done none of that."

Although this case was in the context of trade marks, it highlights the difficulties presented by the internet. It also shows the power of the use of metaphor in this area of law. The irony is that as technology has advanced, the more accessible and easy to understand it has become and this has very often been through the use of metaphor. In developing the law in this area, the same tool of communication is likely to have just as powerful effect on the outcome.

Finally, readers are referred to Chapter 5 for the recent Yahoo! Case in France in which the court found that it had jurisdiction in proceedings against Yahoo! which was not based in that country.

CHAPTER 19

CONSUMER PROTECTION

With the cross-jurisdictional nature of the internet, on-line businesses need to be aware of the consumer protection laws in every jurisdiction in which they are making sales. Consumers will very often be protected in this regard and it is important that both contracting sides are as well-versed as possible in their legal rights.

The following example serves as a warning to those operating in the business-to-consumer market with insufficient legal advice.

> Early in 2000, Microsoft found itself handing out $400 to Californians after it failed to spot a loophole in a special offer for its internet service. In an effort to lure new subscribers to the $22-a-month Microsoft Network (MSN) services, the company had been offering $400 discounts coupons for computers and electrical goods to those willing to sign up to MSN for a full three years. But a poor understanding of California's tight consumer protection laws by Microsoft lawyers meant that locals were able to cancel the service within hours of signing up without penalty. Needless to say, the company quickly suspended the offer after word filtered through that thousands of savvy Silicon Valley consumers were emptying the shelves at electrical superstores of PCs, wide-screen TVs, DVD players and camcorders.

As set out in the last chapter, if a consumer makes a contract on-line or by e-mail from England, it is quite likely that he will be protected by the English consumer protection laws.

This chapter sets out a brief guide to a number of the English consumer protection laws which may potentially apply. In addition to these, the free market has already started providing its own solutions and the final part of this chapter provides a summary of the developments in this area.

BRIEF SUMMARY OF CONCLICT OF LAWS IN THIS AREA

Jurisdiction of English Courts

If the company with which he is contracting is based in either the European Union or a signatory of EFTA, the Civil Jurisdiction and Judgment Acts make clear that a consumer may sue the supplier where either is domiciled. Further, even where the supplier is not domiciled in a contracting state but has a branch, agency or other establishment in a contracting state, he is deemed to be domiciled there. In addition, a consumer may generally only be sued where he is domiciled.

For a supplier based in another country, the English courts will continue to have jurisdiction if the consumer is sued there. They will also have jurisdiction to hear an action against the supplier if the contract was made in England or the breach was committed in England as well as in other certain specific situations such as when the contract was made by or through an agent trading or residing in the jurisdiction.

The issue of where the contract was made will again potentially be an issue and it is possible that a contract actually made on-line may be deemed to have been made when the consumer instantaneously receives the acceptance but where the acceptance was sent when correspondence was by e-mail. These issues are dealt with in the preceding two chapters.

As to where the breach occurred, it is at least arguable that with regard to the delivery of goods this would be where the goods should have been delivered, in other words in England. This issue is dealt with in more detail in the last chapter.

Application of English law

Assuming that the English courts have jurisdiction, the other question which needs answering is whether English law or at least the English consumer protection laws apply. Once again, this is dealt with in detail in the last chapter. Clearly this will be the case if English law is expressly chosen or even if it is the inferred choice. In addition to this, even where an express choice of another law has been made, Article 5(2) makes it clear that in a number of circumstances the consumer will continue to be protected by the 'mandatory rules' of English law.

For these reasons, it is worth setting out a summary of a number of the various consumer protection laws which will potentially apply to consumers making orders from England either on-line or by e-mail.

SUPPLY OF GOODS ACT 1979 ("SGA 79")

Satisfactory quality

Section 14(2) provides that where the seller sells goods in the course of a business, there is an implied term that the goods supplied under the contract are of satisfactory quality. If the goods are not of satisfactory quality, the consumer will have a right either to reject the goods and claim a refund or alternatively to claim damages for breach of contract.

However, it should be noted that the right to reject the goods ends once the goods have been accepted. Section 35 of the SGA 79 provides that acceptance can occur in three ways:

(a) By intimation to the seller that he has accepted them. It should be noted in this regard that section 35(2) provides that where the goods are delivered to the buyer and he has not previously examined them, he is not deemed to have accepted them until he has had a reasonable opportunity of examining them to see if they conform to the terms of the contract. This is so even if the consumer has signed a delivery note;

(b) An act after delivery inconsistent with the seller's ownership; or

(c) Retention beyond a reasonable time. In *Bernstein* v *Pamson Motors (Golders Green)* [1987] 2 All ER 220, the claimant bought a car from the defendant and after three weeks the engine seized up. Rougier J held that by keeping the car for three weeks, the claimant had accepted the car and had therefore lost his right to reject the goods. His remedy lay only in damages which in his case meant a replacement engine.

Reasonable time and price

Section 14 of the SGA 79 also provides that where no time has been agreed for performing the contract, the supplier must perform it within a reasonable time. By section 15 of the SGA 79, where no price has been agreed then a reasonable price must be charged. It should be noted that this does not help a consumer who has agreed to an inflated price. This is treated merely as a bad bargain which is the consumer's responsibility.

SUPPLY OF GOODS AND SERVICES ACT 1982 ("SGSA 82")

Section 13 of the SGSA provides that in a contract for the supply of a service where the supplier in the course of a business, there is an implied term that the supplier will carry out the services with reasonable care and skill.

PRODUCT LIABILITY

If a buyer is injured as a result of a purchase being defective, then he can also claim for his personal injury as well as a claim in contract based upon the purchase not being of satisfactory quality.

Liability may not only be founded in contract and also in the standard law of negligence depending upon the circumstances but also pursuant to the Consumer Protection Act 1987 which implemented the European Communities Directive on Product Liability (85/374).

Section 2(1) of the Act provides that where any damage is caused wholly or partly by a defect in a product, every person to whom subsection (2) applies shall be liable for the damage.

Section 2(2) says that the following persons are primarily liable:

(a) the producer, i.e. the manufacturer;

(b) an own brander who has held himself out as a producer;

(c) the first importer into the European Community.

Where the producer cannot be identified and the supplier is unable to identify anyone further up the chain of supply within a reasonable period of time then the producer will be liable.

Defects are likely to fall into three areas: manufacturing, design and misleading warning notices. The type of damage covered by the Act is specified in section 5 as death, personal injury or damage to private property valued above £275.

Manufacturers have six possible defences to a claim:

(a) the defect was caused by complying with the law;

(b) the manufacturer did not supply the product (e.g. in cases of theft);

(c) the supplier is not in business;

(d) the defect did not exist in the product at the time it was supplied by the producer to another;

(e) the state of scientific and technical knowledge at the relevant time was not such that a producer of products of the same description as the product in question might be expected to have discovered the defect; and

    f.   a producer of a component produced a defective product and the defect was wholly attributable to instructions he had been given by the principal producer. The principal producer would remain potentially liable.

If a defect is discovered by a manufacturer, a recall notice may be made which may reduce any potential damages on the ground of contributory negligence if the consumer carried on using the product when he was aware of the recall.

EXCLUSION CLAUSES

Many contracts contain clauses disclaiming any liability. There are a number of ways in which these may be deemed to be ineffective.

Unfair Contract Terms Act 1977 ("UCTA 77")

This applies where the purchaser is a consumer, so in other words is not acting in the course of a business.

The main provisions of the Act which are relevant to this chapter are that a supplier cannot exclude liability for the following:

    (a) for breach of the obligations under sections 13 and 14 of the SGA 79 and their equivalent provisions in the SGSA 82 (section 6);

    (b) for death or personal injury resulting from negligence (section 2(1));

    (c) for other loss and damage unless the clause is deemed to be reasonable under the Act (sections 2(2) and 11).

With regard to electronic communications, it has already been noted in Chapter 4 above, that section 3 of the Act provides that an exclusion clause which is part of "written" standard terms of business may only be enforced if it satisfies the reasonableness test. So, too, it has been noted that the use of the word written may mean that it does not cover electronic communications.

Unfair Terms in Consumer Contracts Regulations 1999 (SI 1999/2083) ("UTCCR 99")

These Regulations replaced the Unfair Terms in Consumer Contracts Regulations 1994 and implement the E.C. Council Directive on Unfair Terms in Consumer Contracts 93/13/EEC. They apply where the buyer is acting as a consumer and to clauses which have not been individually negotiated, in other words to standard form contracts.

The Regulations provide that if a term to which they apply is 'unfair' then it will be unenforceable as against the consumer. Regulations 5(1) says that a term in unfair if it causes a significant imbalance in the rights and obligations appearing under the contract to the detriment of the consumer contrary to the requirements of good faith. The test is therefore fairness and good faith and a list of possible unfair terms is set out in Schedule 2 of the Regulations.

The other aspect of the Regulations is that they provide that contract terms should be drafted in plain intelligible language and further that any ambiguity will be interpreted in favour of the consumer.

Airlines

A good example of the Regulations is provided by a report in the July Edition of the Office of Fair Trading's ("OFT's") publication, *Fair Trading News*. It reported that airlines had been warned to expect legal action if they did not make scheduled flight contracts fairer to passengers. Non-transferable ticketing, rescheduling of flights without compensation and restrictions on liability for goods damaged were some of 30 airline terms identified by the OFT as potentially unfair and unenforceable. It was argued that the most unfair term of all was that which enabled carriers to prevent consumers from transferring tickets. It was also argued that in practice, the term also obstructs the Package Travel Regulations which enable consumers to nominate another passenger if they are unable to go on holiday themselves.

Package holidays

In the same publication, the OFT reported that in other action on unfair contract terms, UK package holiday companies had received OFT advice on drafting fairer contracts. Prompted by consumer complaints about the loss of prepayments, the level of compensation offered when holidays go wrong, and clauses which seek to limit companies' liability for changes to holidays, the OFT undertook a review of contracts across the industry. The result was a set of guidelines explaining why certain terms would be considered unfair, and suggesting how they could be improved.

Red hand doctrine

A line of common law cases suggests clear and reasonable efforts were not made to bring any particularly onerous and unusual conditions to the attention of the other party if they are to form part of a contract. In one case, Lord Denning used the metaphor of placing a red hand pointing to the onerous clause. See in particular *Interfoto Picture Library* v *Stiletto Visual Programmes* [1989] QB 433, *Thornton* v *Shoe Lane Parking* [1971] 1 All E.R. 686, *McCutcheon* v *David MacBrayne* (1964) C.L.Y. 568 and *Parker* v *South Eastern Ry. Co.* (1877) 2 C.P.D. 416.

This probably does not add much to the UTCCR 99 but it potentially adds another line of attack to such clauses.

Misrepresentation

The general rule is that a contracting party is bound by the words that he has signed. This is called the 'parol evidence' rule. However, potentially, a contract may be re-opened if it was preceded by a misrepresentation or other assurance contrary to the terms of the contract itself.

A misrepresention would make the contract voidable, in other words it may be ended by the party who relied upon that misrepresentation. See *L'Estrange v Graucob* [1934] 2 KB 394, *Couchman v Hill* [1947] 1 KB 554, *Thomas Witter Limited v TBP Industries Limited* [1996] 2 All ER 573.

In addition, it may be argued that the agreement was entered into by the consumer only in consideration of a particular promise by the supplier. Such a promise may potentially:

(a) amount to a separate but related contract called a collateral contract. See *City and Westminster Properties (1934) Ltd v Mudd* [1959] 1 Ch 129 and Lord Denning MR in *J. Evans & Son (Portsmouth) Limited v Andrea Merzario Limited* [1976] 1 WLR 1078.

(b) create an estoppel preventing the hire company from relying on provisions which contradict it. See *City and Westminster Properties (1934) Ltd* (above).

(c) lead a court not to enforce any clause contradicting such a promise on the basis that it is 'repugnant' to it. See Lord Denning MR in *Mendelssohn v Normand* [1970] 1 QB 177.

A recent case which may support the common law arguments for defendants is that of *Carmichael and Leese v National Power PLC (1998), HL* [1999] Lawtel 18 November in which it was held that the construction of documents as a question of law did not apply when the intention of parties, objectively ascertained, had to be gathered partly from documents but also from oral exchanges and conduct. It was then a question of fact. This may help with the use of any oral assurances or representations which may potentially have been made by or on behalf of a hire company.

EXAMPLE

Surf champion Paul Sullivan wishes to buy a surf board from Steve and Jo Pye Surf Shack Limited. He has visited their web-site which advertised a second hand seven foot six mini-mal for £250. He e-mails them asking whether it has ever been previously damaged. The manageress of the surf shack, Rhiannon Jones, replies by e-mail stating that it has not. He therefore e-mails his order. On receipt of the board he discovers that there is evidence to show that the nose of the board has at one time been replaced completely.

Can he claim damages or rescind the contract on the basis of the e-mail from Rhiannon Jones?

CONSUMER CREDIT ACT 1974 ("CCA 74")

The CCA 74 is one of the most technical and convoluted pieces of legislation ever passed. However, it can provide very useful protection against many situations in which credit is provided. It is possible in this book to provide only the very briefest of accounts of some of the provisions. For a fuller exposition, see Professor Goode's comprehensive loose-leaf guide *Consumer Credit Legislation*.

By section 8 of the Act, credit is provided when a debt is deferred. This may be done in a number of ways. It may be a simple loan agreement (usually classified as a 'debtor-creditor' ("DC") agreement) or a loan specifically made to finance the provision of goods or services. If there is an agreement between the creditor and the supplier, such a loan will generally constitute a 'debtor-creditor-supplier' ("DCS") agreement. Depending upon the circumstances, it may occasionally constitute a DC agreement.

If the loan is for between £100 and £25,000 and between accompany and an individual (which includes partnerships but not companies), the agreement will be regulated by the Act subject to certain exemption provision concerning short-term credit, a small number of instalments and low rates of interest. If the agreement is regulated, it must include a host of notices of the protections and remedies available to the consumer. Most people will have seen such an agreement when they have signed up for a credit card agreement. If the agreement does not contain these provisions then it is unenforceable against the consumer without an order of the court.

If, as is common with on-line transactions, the agreement was not made at the premises of the creditor and it was preceded by oral antecedent negotiations by or on behalf of the creditor, it may be a 'cancellable' agreement giving the debtor a cooling-off period of one week. If a cancellation notice is not included in such an agreement then it will be unenforceable in all circumstances.

As well as credit agreements, the Act also covers hire agreements where the hire is capable of subsisting for more than three months (section 15 of the Act). Once again, if the agreement is regulated the various formalities need to be complied with.

It should be noted that the Act may well apply to many more areas than people perhaps expect. There has been very little case law on the Act but recently it has come to the fore concerning disputes between the insurance and credit hire industries culminating in the cases of *Dimond* v *Lovell* [2000] 2 W.L.R. 1121 and *Zoan* v *Rouamba* [2000] 1 W.L.R. 1509.

Potentially, internet service providers may be providing instalment credit. Mobile phone providers may be providing either instalment credit or consumer hire agreement. If travel companies have a buy now, pay later offer, this may also be the provision of credit covered by the Act depending upon the circumstances.

Perhaps the most important implication of the Act for transactions by e-mail or on-line involve credit card purchases of goods or services.

Standard credit cards would generally involve a three-party DCS agreement for what the Act describes as 'restricted-use' credit. For this type of agreement, if the value of the transaction is between £100 and £30,000 and it is regulated, section 75 of the Act will apply. In these circumstances, not only would the supplier be liable for any breach of contract but the creditor would also be so liable. This is particularly helpful to debtors where, for example, the supplier has gone into liquidation or is being particularly unhelpful or difficult to contact.

In these circumstances the credit card company will be liable for not only breaches of contract by the supplier but also for any misrepresentation by them. It should be noted that certain types of credit card companies such as American Express and Diner's Club provide exempt agreements under the Act and therefore would not be so liable.

The Director General of Fair Trading and the Department of Trade and Industry are the enforcement authorities for the Act.

EXAMPLE

Yorkshire Dales farmers Lorna and Bruce Wilson order a football video from football specialist Dean Norton Football Supplies. They order by e-mail using their credit card provided by French Bank Credite Helene Piquion SA. Unfortunately, on delivery the video is defective and in breach of the contract made with Dean Norton Football Supplies.

Is their credit card company equally liable with Dean Norton Football Supplies for the defective video?

OTHER REGULATORY PROVISIONS

There are numerous regulatory and statutory provisions regulating consumer transactions and it would not be possible to list them all in this book. However, it is worth being aware that the following exist.

Trade Descriptions Act 1968

This makes it an offence, subject to various defences, in the course of a business to apply a false trade description or to supply or offer to supply goods to which a false trade description is applied.

The Package Travel Package Holidays and Package Tours Regulations 1992

These implemented European Directive 90/314 and provide, among other things, that package organisers or retailers shall not supply any descriptive matter concerning the package which mislead the consumer. If they do, they will be liable to compensate the consumer for any loss which the consumer suffers in consequence. Further, the organiser and/or retailer is strictly liable for the proper performance of the obligations under the contract whether or not they are providing the service or whether such services are to be provided by other suppliers.

Contracts (Rights of Third Parties) Act 1999

This provides that subject to various provisions, a person who is not a party to a contract may in his own right enforce a term of the contract if either the contract expressly provides that he may or if the term purports to confer a benefit on him subject to the proviso that if on a proper construction of the contract it appears that the parties did not intend the term to be enforceable by the third party. This will have the effect of giving explicit rights to those on for example a holiday who were not parties to the contract of purchase of the holiday.

Misleading prices

Part III of the Consumer Protection Act 1987 makes it an offence to give consumers a misleading price indication about goods, services or accommodation. Guidance may also be found in the Price marking Order 1991 which was made under the Prices Act 1974 and implements two European Directives 88/314 and 88/315.

Distance Selling Regulations

The Consumer Protection (Distance Selling) Regulations 2000 (SI 2000/2334) implemented the Council Directive on the protection of consumers in respect of distance contracts (97/7/EC) ("the Distance Selling Directive").

The Regulations apply to contracts for goods or services to be supplied to a consumer where the contract is made exclusively by means of distance communication, that is any means used without the simultaneous physical presence of the consumer and the supplier (regulations 3 and 4). Schedule 1 contains an indicative list of means of distance communication which includes e-mail. The Regulations do not apply to those distance contracts excluded by regulation 5(1), such as contracts relating to the supply of financial services.

The Regulations have limited application to contracts for the supply of groceries by regular delivery and contracts for the provision of accommodation, transport, catering or leisure services (regulation 6).

The Regulations require the supplier to provide the consumer with the information referred to in regulation 7 prior to the conclusion of the contract. This includes information on the right to cancel the distance contract, the main characteristics of the goods or services, and delivery costs where appropriate.

Regulation 8 requires the supplier to confirm in writing, or another durable medium which is available and accessible to the consumer, information already given and to give some additional information, including information on the conditions and procedures relating to the exercise of the right to cancel the contract. Regulation 8(3) requires the supplier to inform the consumer prior to conclusion of a contract for services that he will not be able to cancel once performance of the service has begun with his agreement.

Where the Regulations apply, they provide a "cooling off period" to enable the consumer to cancel the contract by giving notice of cancellation to the supplier. The effect of giving notice of cancellation under the Regulations is that the contract is treated as if it had not been made.

Where the supplier supplies the information to the consumer on time, the cooling-off period is seven working days from the day after the date of the contract, in the case of services, or from the day after the date of delivery of the goods. Where the supplier fails to comply with the information requirement at all, the cooling-off period is extended by 3 months. Where the supplier complies with the information requirement later than he should have done but within 3 months the cooling-off begins from the date he provided the information (regulations 10–12). Certain contracts are excluded from the right to cancel unless the parties agree otherwise, such as a contract for the supply of goods made to the consumer's specifications (regulation 13).

If the consumer cancels, the consumer must be reimbursed within a maximum period of 30 days (regulation 14). Where the consumer cancels the contract, any related credit agreement is automatically cancelled (regulation 15). Regulation 17 provides that on cancellation of the contract the consumer is under a duty to restore goods to the supplier if he collects them and in the meantime to take reasonable care of them. The Regulations do not require the consumer to return goods but if he is required to under the contract and does not do so, he must pay the cost to the supplier of recovering them.

The Regulations provide that the contract must be performed within 30 days subject to agreement between the parties. However, where the supplier is not able to provide the goods or service ordered, substitutes may be offered if certain conditions are met (regulation 19).

The Regulations provide that where the consumer's payment card is used fraudulently in connection with a distance contract the consumer will be entitled to cancel the payment. If the payment has already been made the consumer will be entitled to a re-credit or to have all sums returned by the card issuer. The Regulations amend the Consumer Credit Act 1974 by removing the potential liability of the debtor under a regulated consumer credit agreement for the first £50 of loss to the creditor from misuse of a credit-token in connection with a distance contract.

The Regulations prohibit the supply of unsolicited goods and services to consumers. Regulation 24 replaces with amendments section 1 of the Unsolicited Goods and Services Act 1971 and Article 3 of the Unsolicited Goods and Services (Northern Ireland) Order 1976. It also creates an offence in similar terms to section 2 of the 1971 Act but extended to the supply of unsolicited services and limited to supply to consumers. The scope of section 2 of the 1971 Act and Article 4 of the 1976 Order (which apply only to goods) is amended to restrict their application to the unsolicited supply of goods to businesses.

The Director General of Fair Trading, Trading Standards Departments in Great Britain and the Department of Enterprise, Trade and Investment in Northern Ireland are enforcement authorities for the purposes of the Regulations. Regulation 26 provides that an enforcement authority must consider complaints about a breach of the requirements of the Regulations. Those bodies are given the power to take proceedings for an injunction against a business to prevent further breaches (regulation 27).

CONSUMER WEB-SITES

There are a number of web-sites devoted to protecting the consumer rights. The following are provided by way of example.

For on-line and off-line consumers

Many consumer organisations now have web-sites.

(a) *www.tradingstandards.gov.uk:* Trading Standards Institute

(b) *www.tradingstandards.net:* includes a notice boards for complaints

(b) *www.bbc.co.uk/watchdog:* BBC's Watchdog

(c) *www.ofthelp.com:* Office of Fair Trading's official web-site

(d) *www.which.net:* Which? magazine

(e) *www.lawrights.co.uk:* legal questions and answers

On-line consumers

In response to the lack of consumer confidence in e-commerce, a number of sights have developed in order to counteract this. In their different ways they claim to act as a quality control for web-traders.

(a) *www.uktrust.co.uk:* Code of Practice and icon for approved sites

(b) *www.which.net/webtrader/index.html:* Code of Practice and icon for approved sites

(c) *www.shopsafe.co.uk:* offers access to sites it deems secure

(d) *www.netconsumer.net:* includes discussion forums, chat rooms and recommended sites

CHAPTER 20

FUTURE INTERNATIONAL HARMONISATION

As with most aspects of e-mail law at present, the issues identified with regard to e-commerce raise more questions than they answer. The Electronic Communications Act 2000 was a bold step down the line of creating a new body of law but it remains to be seen whether the legislative process can keep up with the developments in the internet. Otherwise the straight-jacket of the common law will have to be loosened to allow for the changes ahead.

This chapter sets out some of the more recent international developments which potentially point the way to future developments.

THE E-COMMERCE DIRECTIVE

Perhaps the most important aspect of future legal change is the European Union's Electronic Commerce Directive 2000/31/EC, L178; [2000] OJ 17 July (*http://europa.eu.int/comm/internal_market/en/media/eleccomm/com31en.pdf*). This seeks to contribute to the proper functioning of the internal market by ensuring the free movement of information society services between the member states.

In order to achieve that objective it approximates certain national provisions on information society services relating to the internal market, the establishment of service providers, commercial communications, electronic contracts, the liability of intermediaries, codes of conduct, out-of-court dispute settlements, court actions and cooperation between the Member States. Member States are obliged to bring into force the laws, regulations and administrative provisions necessary to comply with this Directive not later than 17 January 2002.

Before 17 July 2003, and at two-yearly intervals after that date, the Commission will submit to the European Parliament, the Council and the Economic and Social Committee, a report on the application of the Directive, accompanied where necessary, by proposals for adapting it to legal, technical and economic developments in the field of information technology services, in particular with regard to crime prevention, the protection of children and consumer protection.

Scope of the Directive

The Directive covers all Information Society services, both business to business and business to consumer, and services provided free of charge to the recipient (e.g. funded by advertising or sponsorship revenue and services allowing for on-line electronic transactions such as tele-shopping and on-line shopping malls). The sectors and activities covered include on-line newspapers, on-line databases, on-line financial services, on-line professional services (such as lawyers, doctors, accountants, estate agents), on-line entertainment services (such as video on demand) on-line direct marketing, on-line advertising and other on-line services.

The Directive applies only to service providers established within the E.U. However, the Directive takes care to avoid incompatibility and inconsistency with legal developments in other parts of the world in order to minimise obstacles to global electronic commerce.

Establishment

Article 2(c) of the Directive defines the place of establishment of a service provider as the place where the operator actually pursues an economic activity using a fixed establishment. The establishment of a service provider is therefore irrespective of where web-sites or servers are situated or where the operator may have a mail box. Article 3 requires that providers of information society services should (bar a number of exceptions) be subject to the laws of the Member State in which they are established.

Article 4 of the Directive prohibits Member States from imposing special authorisation schemes for Information Society services. Article 5 requires Member States to oblige Information Society service providers to make available to customers and competent authorities basic information concerning their activities, including their name, address, e-mail address, trade register number, professional authorisation and membership of professional bodies where applicable, and their VAT number.

On-line Contracts

Article 9 requires Member States to remove any prohibitions or restrictions on the use of electronic contracts. Articles 10 and 11 impose certain information requirements for the conclusion of electronic contracts, in particular in order to help consumers to avoid technical errors.

Liability of Intermediaries

Article 12 requires Member States to ensure that service providers are not liable for the content of communications in cases where they play a passive role as a "mere conduit" of information from third parties. Articles 13 and 14 limit service providers' liability for other intermediary activities such as the storage of information.

Commercial Communications

Article 2(f) of the Directive defines commercial communications (such as advertising and direct marketing). Articles 6 makes these communications subject to certain transparency requirements to ensure consumer confidence and fair trading. As mentioned in Chapter 9, above, Article 7 requires that commercial communications by e-mail are clearly identifiable. Article 8 lays down that, with regard to regulated professions (such as lawyers or accountants), the on-line provision of services is permitted and national rules on advertising shall not prevent these professions from operating web-sites. However, Article 8 requires that the on-line activities of regulated professions will have to respect certain rules of professional ethics which should be reflected in codes of conduct to be drawn up by professional associations.

Implementation

The Directive seeks to strengthen mechanisms to ensure that existing EU and national legislation is enforced. Article 16 requires the development of codes of conduct at EU level; Article 19 requires administrative co-operation between Member States; Article 17 requires the setting-up of effective, alternative cross-border on-line dispute settlement systems; Article 18 requires Member States to provide for fast, efficient legal redress appropriate to the on-line environment; and Article 20 requires Member States to ensure that sanctions for violations of the rules established under the Directive are effective, proportionate and dissuasive.

Restrictions

The Directive does not deal with the application of the Brussels Convention on jurisdiction, recognition and enforcement of judgments in civil and commercial matters. The Directive does not interfere with the Rome Convention as regards the law applicable to contractual obligations in consumer contracts or with the freedom of the parties to choose the law applicable to their contract. On a case by case basis, Member States will be allowed to impose restrictions on Information Society services supplied from another Member States where this is necessary to protect the public interest regarding the protection of minors, the fight against hatred on grounds of race, sex, religion or nationality, public health or security and consumer protection. However, any such restrictions will have to be proportionate to the stated objective, and can only be imposed after the Member State in which the service provider is established has been asked to take adequate measures and has failed to do so.

UK implementation

Member States now have until 16 January 2002 to implement the requirements of the Directive. The UK will need to take a number of actions to ensure compliance with the Directive. These actions include:

- Checking that UK legislation does not restrict the provision of Information Society services from other Member States;

- Ensuring the existence of appropriate enforcement powers;

- Developing administrative guidance to govern commercial use of the internet by regulated professions;

- Checking for restrictions that might hinder the conclusion of contracts on-line;

- Checking legislation to ensure that service providers are not liable for the content of communications which they transmit for third parties;

- Encouraging the development of codes of conduct to contribute to implementation of the Directive;

- Developing guidance for organisations providing alternative dispute resolution services on-line;

- Identifying, resourcing and promoting a UK contact point to facilitate co-operation with Member States and with the Commission.

In Autumn 2000, the Department of Trade and Industry published a public consultation document requiring replies by 1 April 2001. It stated that the Government was committed to introducing legislation in the current Parliamentary session. The consultation document may be found at:

www.dti.gov.uk/cii/ecommerce/ukecommercestrategy/archiveconsultation-docs/index.shtml

DRAFT REGULATION ON ENFORCEMENT OF CIVIL AND COMMERCIAL JUDGMENTS

This was a proposal for a European Union Council Regulation on Jurisdiction and the Recognition and Enforcement of Judgments in Civil and Commercial Matters COM (99) 348 final (Commission of the European Communities Documents – 14 July 1999) (*http://www.europa.eu.int/eur-lex/en/com/pdf/1999/en_599PC0348.pdf*). Its purpose is to harmonise the rules of private international law relating to jurisdiction and to improve the recognition and enforcement of judgments in civil and commercial matters. It would replace and update the Brussels Convention of 1968 (and its Protocol) in order to take account of new forms of commerce which did not exist in 1968.

In response to this the Department of Trade and Industry held a public consultation (*http://www.dti.gov.uk/cacp/ca/ecommerce.htm*) in Spring 2000. The main focus of the consultation was on-line consumer contracts and the need to up-date the rules in this area in particular with reference to Article 5 of the Rome Convention and Article 13 of the Brussels Convention. Legislation is now awaited.

UNIFORM COMMERCIAL CODE

The American Uniform Commercial Code has made an attempt to try and unify some of these issues. In particular, section 2B – 108 provides:

"(a) A choice-of-law term in an agreement is enforceable.
(b) If an agreement does not have a choice-of-law term, the following rules apply:
  (1) In an access contract or a contract providing for delivery of a copy by electronic communication, the contract is governed by the law of the jurisdiction in which the licensor is located when the contract becomes unenforceable between the parties.
  (2) A consumer contract not governed by subsection (b) (1) which requires delivery of a copy on a physical medium to the consumer is governed as to the contractual rights and obligations of the parties by the law of the jurisdiction in which the copy is located when the licensee receives possession of the copy or, in the event of non-delivery, the jurisdiction in which the receipt was to have occurred.
  (3) In all other cases, the contract is governed by the law of the State with the most significant relationship to the contract.
(c) If the jurisdiction whose law applies as determined under subsection (b) is outside the United States, subsection (b) applies only if the laws of that jurisdiction provide substantially similar protections and rights to the party not located in that jurisdiction as are provided under this article. Otherwise, the rights and duties of the parties are governed by the law of the jurisdiction in the United States which has the most significant relationship to the transaction.
(d) A party is located at its place of business if it has one place of business, at its chief executive office if it has more than one place of business, or at its place of incorporation or primary registration if it does not have a physical place of business. Otherwise, a party is located at its primary residence."

Unfortunately, this Code is only applicable to those states in which it has been enacted and even then only with regard to the United States and its commonwealth.

UNCITRAL MODEL LAW ON ELECTRONIC COMMERCE

UNCITRAL, the UN body most concerned with electronic commerce, has for some time been working on the legal consequences of the development of electronic commerce. In 1996 the Model Law on Electronic Commerce (www.uncitral.org/en-index.htm) was finalised. It comprises model provisions for legislators to adopt when considering how to make sure that electronic commerce is legally recognised. The Model Law covers, for example, the legal recognition of electronic writing and signatures. More recently a working group has been undertaking more detailed work on Uniform Rules on electronic signatures and certification authorities. Amongst other issues, the rules note the requirement for standards to be met for Certification Authorities issuing certificates used for legal recognition, and the need for mutual recognition of "trusted" certificates on a global basis.

PART 5: CONCLUSION

CHAPTER 21
CONCLUSION

"Now he was master of the world, and he was not quite sure what to do next. But he would think of something."

Arthur C. Clarke, 2001: a space odyssey

At present, the law in this area consists of an amorphous collection of rules from numerous specialised disciplines. However, there can be little doubt that in years to come the law of e-mail will itself be regarded as a separate and distinct discipline in the study of law.

The contents of this guide highlight the tension referred to in Chapter 1 between the competing principles of freedom and regulation. Beyond that it offers a cautionary note for the unwary. Like it or not, the internet is already regulated and those that fail to recognise this, be they individuals or companies, do so at their peril.

As to the future, the development of the law will largely depend upon the development of e-mail and the internet, both in its technology and its commercialisation. Change in this area will probably come to be viewed as a constant and users of e-mail will need to keep abreast of such change.

It is hoped that this guide provides a useful contribution to this process.

E-MAIL AND THE LAW

– essential knowledge for safer surfing

Truly the first comprehensive guide to the legal implications involved with the use of e-mail. This easy to read book is aimed at all those using e-mail and other forms of electronic communication ranging from the consumer and small business to large corporations, lawyers and specialists. It highlights the potential pitfalls which may beset the unwary and assuages the curiosity of all those taking an interest in this developing area of law.

Tim Kevan is a Barrister at 1 Temple Gardens (www.1templegardens.co.uk) with expertise in computer, consumer, employment and personal injury law. He studied economics and law at Magdalene College, Cambridge University and was a scholar of the Middle Temple. In 1993, he was awarded a Young European of the Year Award (Stiftung FVS Joseph Bech Travel Scholarship) by M. Jacques Santer, former President of the European Commission. He has a long-standing interest in the relationship between law and the internet and drafted the Bar's Practice Standards for the use of e-mail by the Bar in 1997. He is the author of the textbook: *A Guide to Credit Hire and Repair: Law and Practice* (1999, CLT Professional Publishing), the Second Edition of which is due in 2001. He surfs and mountain-bikes near his home town of Minehead in Somerset and supports Manchester City. Contact: *timkevan@1templegardens.co.uk.*

Paul McGrath is also a Barrister at 1 Temple Gardens with expertise in computer, employment, consumer and personal injury law. He studied law at London University and was a scholar of Gray's Inn. Contact: *paulmcgrath@1templegardens.co.uk.*

INDEX